Running from the Devil

Running from the Devil

A Memoir of a Boy Possessed

Steve Kissing

A CROSSROAD BOOK
THE CROSSROAD PUBLISHING COMPANY
NEW YORK ◆ BERKELEY

The Crossroad Publishing Company
481 Eighth Avenue, New York, NY 10001

Printed in the United States of America

Library of Congress Cataloging-in-Publication Data

Kissing, Steve.
   Running from the devil : a memoir of a boy possessed / Steve Kissing.
      p. cm.
"A Crossroad Carlisle book."
   ISBN 0-8245-2105-6
      1. Kissing, Steve—Childhood and youth. 2. Epileptic children—United States—Biography. 3. Catholics—United States—Biography. I. Title.
BX4705.K57 A3 2003
248.8'6196853'0092—dc21

2002015199

1 2 3 4 5 6 7 8 9 10 09 08 07 06 05 04 03

The following trademarks are mentioned in this book:
Coke®, Blow Pop®, Cracker Jack®, Earth Shoes® , Gatorade®, Jell-O®, M&M's®, Nike®, Pet Rocks ®, Pop-Tarts®, STP®, Wheaties®, Wonder Bread®

The photo on page 45 comes courtesy of Larry Flynt, self-proclaimed "Defender of the First Amendment."

B. Kissing

Contents

A Word from the Author

What follows is a true story about my thoroughly weird, though oddly wonderful, childhood. You should know, however, that the tale is driven almost entirely by imagination and memory. *My* imagination and *my* memory. Though I relied some on letters, journals, and other mementos, I did not place my recollections before friends and family for a vote. To borrow a phrase from Tobias Wolff, "memory has its own story to tell."

I have also *deliberately* altered some facts. The reasons for this are both legal and literary. For instance, I have changed most people's names. Some events are presented out of order. And I did create a couple of composite characters.

In short, this is not a work of journalism. But while certain details in this story may not be precisely factual, the sense of what was in my mind and my heart is *absolutely* true. As is the fact that, while growing up, I somehow managed to keep a big and scary secret all to myself. At first, it's a hard thing to believe. I know. But, on closer inspection, mine is but one of countless cases in which children go to great lengths to hide, disguise, or even intentionally misinterpret what troubles and bewilders them. What child doesn't enjoy imagining a world that is somehow better, be it more safe or sensitive, more friendly or fantastic?

Finally, I wish to emphasize that I am not a physician. Or a theologian. Nor were any consulted in the preparation of this book.

I hope you enjoy my story.

Steve Kissing
Cincinnati, Ohio
Fall 2002

To Mom, not only funnier, better.
To Dad, not only faster, better.

Chapter 1

A Day to Remember

I knew what it felt like to pretend that the teacher had a pie in her face, that a girl had a beard, or that a priest was a Russian spy, the cross around his neck a camera beaming pictures back to the Kremlin. As such, when I had my first hallucination I knew that the horribly strange stuff in my head was not of my doing.

Some days are made for remembering. Like the day when you first learn how to ride a two-wheeler. Or, in my case, the day I and everyone else in my second-grade class saw Suzie Littlementh nearly naked. She was dressing for gym when the fire alarm sounded. She ran outside wearing nothing but her white go-go boots and pink panties. One doesn't forget a day like that. And I certainly have not forgotten the first day that someone or something came out of nowhere and took control of my mind.

On that day, I was an eleven-year-old fifth-grader at St. William, one of several Catholic elementary schools in the working-class Cincinnati neighborhood of Price Hill. The year was 1974. My favorite football team, the Miami Dolphins, won their second straight Super Bowl, thanks largely to Bob Griese and Larry Csonka. Ray Stevens' "The Streak," was my favorite song. And the adults all seemed to be talking about Watergate, whatever that was.

The day I first lost control of my mind was typical fifth-grade fare: homeroom, reading, history, and gym in the morning. Then a lunch of peas, canned ravioli, and fruit cocktail entombed in green gelatin. Recess was spent trying to outrun the guy covering me in tag football. It was then on to religion, math, and social studies.

That otherwise ordinary October day was deceptively sunny. My mind, like that of every other kid in the building, was intently focused on playing outside after school. The urge to enjoy the outdoors was at its zenith. The sun's bright rays recalled summer past, but the sun's low position reminded us that shorter, darker days were coming. The day, no doubt heaven-sent, was the kind when you played and played until your mom begged and begged you to come home for dinner.

Without warning of any sort, I began to hallucinate in social studies, smack in the middle of a tricky pop quiz on American Indians. One moment I was trying to remember the various ways the Red Man used maize; the next moment my brain felt as if it were tossed into one of those domed dice tumblers in the middle of a board game, some angry person pounding it over and over, dissatisfied with every number.

Everything registered as something other than who or what it really was. David McKinley, seated to my right, continued to look like himself, but my mind identified him as my thirty-five-year-old Uncle Lloyd. Kim Lacey, to my left, didn't physically change either (nor did I ever want her to), but my mind convinced me she

2

was pop singer Helen Reddy. The pencil holder on the teacher's desk became a shovel; the film strip machine, a tuba; the corner coat rack, a big strip of bacon. And the blackboard became a hypodermic needle, blood on the tip.

I heard voices, too—startling voices, as when adults argue in the next room. The voices shouted in English, I think, but their speech was garbled, like when someone tries to talk with a mouthful of potato chips.

And I felt my brain change as if the soft tissue was turning to concrete from the inside out. My scalp tingled, and I would have sworn my hairs were standing on end, tiny sparks frolicking around my follicles. Never before could I recall actually feeling my brain. It creeped me out worse than the time when Carol Dank had a nosebleed and the teacher had her stand above the aquarium, the fish rising to the surface to sip her blood.

The experience, which lasted only seconds, seemed much longer. It was as if Time had been sucker-punched in the stomach and was now bent over, heaving, trying to recapture its breath and its dignity. (A position not unfamiliar to me.) The disturbance left as quickly as it came, zooming away like the Starship *Enterprise* after Captain Kirk orders the engines pushed to Warp 6.

The totally unexpected and freaky nature of what I experienced had the same effect on me as the nasty bicycle crash I had a few months earlier. I was zooming down the sidewalk faster than ever before, 100-percent pleased to be alive, pretending that I was piloting an airplane above a dense jungle, dropping napalm on the enemy. And then without warning, my front wheel hung up on something and I was kissing concrete, my palms, knees, and nose all losing some skin. I was no longer the carefree airplane pilot, but a villager down below, my skin on fire.

The episode in school left me with a C-minus on the quiz and a creepy feeling that stubbornly clung to me, like a Cracker Jack tattoo, for days. When the bell rang that day, I bolted out of the building, my mind racing, my young heart full of fear. Despite the sun and the warm fall breeze, I was in no mood for the usual after-school adventures with buddies Greg Teal, Lou Bella, and Kevin Craine. I just wanted to get home. *Fast.*

I spent the rest of the day on high alert, expecting the sensation to return. In fact, I hoped it would. Another episode wouldn't catch me off guard, I reasoned, so I'd be in a better position to analyze it.

I waited, too, for Mom or Dad to notice that something wasn't right with me. Married in their teens and only a few years older when they had me, they were young and as hip as parents could possibly be. And perceptive, too. I never had to tell them when I wasn't feeling well or when I was reprimanded for acting up in class; Mom and Dad could *always* tell. Surely, they would see *this.*

But my parents didn't notice that night. And I couldn't bring myself to tell them. How could I put into words something so odd, so troublesome, so downright frightening? The words were nowhere to be found. Besides, the adults in my life would have assumed that I was telling another one of my fibs.

Back in second grade, I told my teacher that my mother was expecting, for it seemed as if all the other students' mothers were pregnant. When my classmates brought in pictures of newborns wrapped tight in hospital blankets, I brought in a tale about my mother's miscarriage. I told the story so convincingly that the teacher gave me a sympathy card to give to my mother. And I was dumb enough to give it to her.

But the hallucination was not the work of my imagination. Of that much I was absolutely certain. I considered exaggeration—in all its forms—one of my greatest talents. Maybe my only one. Adults often praised my creativity. And my friends enjoyed my storytelling, especially when the antagonist was Bloody Bones, the rickety skeleton who patrolled our school at night, tormenting any student foolish enough to stay behind.

I told my best Bloody Bones stories in dark closets on rainy Saturday afternoons. My face, taut with exaggerated strain and partially illuminated by the beam of a dim flashlight, made believers of everyone who heard my yarn.

So I knew what it meant to imagine something that wasn't—and maybe even *couldn't* be—true. I knew what it felt like to pretend that the teacher had a pie in her face, that a girl had a beard, or that a priest was a Russian spy, the cross around his neck a camera beaming pictures back to the Kremlin. As such, when I had my first hallucination I knew that the horribly strange stuff in my head was not of my doing. It was not pretend. It was not a dream. No, it was as real as my orange-and-black bike with the banana seat. As real as my school desk with the flip-up lid. As real as my love for rockets, race cars, and reading.

But what was the cause? *Everything* had one.

There was nothing unusual about the day. I had risen early and eaten a bowl of oatmeal with my siblings: Larry, a seventh grader; Dave, in third grade; and Teri, in second. We didn't talk while we shoveled the oats into our mouths and listened to Top-40 tunes on WSAI-AM. Carly Simon's "You're So Vain" and Jim Croce's "Bad, Bad Leroy Brown" were included in that morning's play list. We then walked, along with our cousins Mike and Lisa, who lived below us in our two-family home, to St. William, a half-mile away. The rest of the day prior to the hallucination was also too ordinary to provide any clues.

But there must be some explanation, I thought. My favorite subject was science. Great minds figured out gravity, molecules, and how to make soft-serve ice cream, so certainly I could unlock this mystery of mine. For a week, my mission in life was determining what happened to my head to cause my condition.

5

My fifth grade photo. The piece of notebook paper in my pocket was my lame attempt at mimicking the sophisticated look of a kerchief in a suit pocket.

Three likely possibilities came to mind—three incidents that each left me with tremendous headaches. Perhaps one or more injured my brain.

Possible Cause #1: That previous summer I left my eye glasses, thick as bullet-proof glass, at home rather than risk ridicule wearing them at week-long camp. I walked off the trail several times into thick brush, but at least I wasn't called "four eyes." By the time my parents picked up my siblings and me, abrasions covered my arms and legs. And I was vomiting from the eyestrain.

Possible Cause #2: While exploring the innards of an electric alarm clock—which I had failed to unplug—my metal screwdriver touched the power coil. A heavy jolt shot up my arm, dropping my skinny body, then topped with long, brown hair, to the floor. I lost a good five minutes of my life to that clock.

Possible Cause #3: In an attempt to understand how a light bulb works, I stared into one that was illuminated for fifteen minutes. The burning sensation in the back of my eyes and the headache that lasted for hours were a small price to pay for the pursuit of scientific truth.

I dismissed these possible causes. Each had happened at least three months prior, a long time ago, and there had been no immediate side effects.

The disturbing hallucinations and eerie sensations would return several times during the next couple of months. Through devotion to my science project (a papier-mâché volcano powered by vinegar and baking soda) as well as overdoses of board games, I managed for those few months to mostly ignore my troubled condition, whatever its sorry cause. I did come close to saying something once or twice, but as with before, I struggled to find the right words. I feared it was something bad. Real bad. I knew for sure when the hallucinations began happening in God's house.

Chapter 2

Murder and Mayhem

My stomach felt queasy as I trudged out of the pew and toward the door with the rest of my class. That day would forever change things. I would divide my life in two parts: BD and AD. Before Devil and After Devil.

Each week, the students at St. William's Elementary attended Mass. I did my best to make sense of what I saw and heard, creating my own interpretations to fill in any blanks. For me, the Bible symbolized God, the crucifixes represented Jesus, and the puffs of smoke from burning candles or incense were a reminder of the Holy Ghost, perfectly named because he was the hardest of the Trinity to imagine.

Though the words—let alone the theology—of the Mass were largely beyond our understanding, we welcomed the mandatory weekday worship, because the hour that Mass required shortened all of our classes. Ten minutes subtracted from math class was a blessing in its own right, one appreciated by us kids as much as, if not more than, the opportunity to partake in God's meal.

There was much to enjoy inside St. William, a large, sandstone church reminiscent of the great European cathedrals, not to mention the Vatican's Basilica of St. Peter, which I had seen in encyclopedias. St. William's Church featured massive Italian marble pillars, always cool to the touch, even in August; one-

St. William's Church, Price Hill.

hundred-foot ceilings, way taller than any tree my friends and I had ever climbed; and angels painted high above the main altar, right where you would expect the real ones to be fluttering about.

I also enjoyed the statues inside St. William. There was one of Jesus, of course, his sacred heart exposed, a sword through it with a flame coming out of the top. There were also statues of Mary and Joseph. I especially liked how the banks of votive candles at the base of these religious replicas cast flickering shadows on their ceramic faces, which usually made them look as if they were crying for our sins. But every now and then, they looked as if they were laughing at us.

What Jesus and his parents found so funny, I wasn't absolutely sure. Maybe it was seventh-grade teacher Mrs. Lauderman's tie-dyed dress. Or the fact that you could see Frank Lucinda's underwear when he genuflected before stepping into the pew.

I especially liked all the textures and colors of the Mass: the priest's silky purple robes, the smooth gold chalices, and the waxy wooden pews polished to a glorious shine. Mass was always a good show.

I felt safe inside St. William, too. Only one place compared: my parents' bed. As a younger child, I sought refuge between Mom and Dad when evening thunderstorms rocked our house—

and my nerves. I was invincible when between parents or pews. Or so I thought.

On this particular day, about two months after my initial hallucination, the drama of Mass took on new proportions when, right after Communion, reality contorted like the horribly disfigured fingers of ninety-five-year-old Sister Mary James. Without warning, it was as if I had been beamed to another planet where things looked just as they did on earth, but meant something else altogether.

In this new and bizarre world—one I would visit often in the coming years—if you looked up "altar," for example, in the dictionary, the definition would read exactly as it did back on earth, but the accompanying picture would be a cougar or a doorknob or a piece of apple pie. During this particular visit, the Blessed Virgin still looked like the Blessed Virgin, but my mind convinced me she was a refrigerator. The organ looked like an organ, but my mind told me it was mailbox. And, strangest of all, Father Kennedy, our beloved pastor, looked as he usually did, but my mind convinced me he was Abraham Lincoln.

The sensation in my head returned. The flesh and blood in my skull felt like a piece of machinery, its gears grinding, its base vibrating, steam hissing out its sides. The sounds of the Mass—the music, the priests' pronouncements, kids sneezing—were alternately sped up and slowed down, just as if I spun a portion of a 45 rpm record at 33 rpm's and then 78 rpm's.

After regaining control of my mind, I was frightened like I had never been before or since. And then—right then—is when I, with a predisposition toward the fanciful and imaginary, leapt to a conclusion that would set off a crazy chain of events and alter the way I looked at myself, the world, everything.

I concluded that only one being could possibly have the power to penetrate the protective force field of St. William's Church and play pranks upon the faithful in God's own home. It was then—right then—when I realized that I was possessed by the Devil himself.

God have mercy on my poor soul!

Who other than Satan could cause such nerve-wracking, stomach-churning experiences? Who else would dare interfere with the beauty, pageantry, and mystery of the Holy Mass? Who else would dare mess with Father Kennedy, President Lincoln, and especially the Mother of God, the Blessed Virgin herself? Only Satan had that kind of nerve.

The Devil wasn't some figment of my imagination. Nor was he a symbolic representation of evil and eternal damnation that the church concocted to keep us kids in line. Sure, he had that effect on us, at least most of the time, but he was a real being, capable of interfering in human affairs, capable of turning most anyone into his plaything.

The fact that Satan would target me was, unfortunately, not hard to grasp. I'd been asking for trouble. "Do bad things and you befriend the Devil," Sister Lucy had told us. She was one of our teachers who belonged to the Sisters of Charity, a dozen of whom lived in a convent on school grounds. Sister Lucy was always smiling, the gold crucifix around her neck always shining, even on cloudy days. Some sort of miracle, I supposed.

The nuns were women beyond reproach. So Sister Lucy was right about the Devil. She was right about *everything*.

And I had been a naughty boy. No doubt about that.

I shoplifted candy bars from the neighborhood pharmacy and convenience stores. I stole coins from the lunch money jar Mom kept atop the refrigerator. I made gunpowder with Lou Bella after being told by Mom that if she ever caught me with the banned substance, she'd rip my limbs off. One by one.

But as I quickly inventoried these and my other sins, while acting as if I was paying attention to the Mass, my biggest transgression leapt out of my subconscious. It stood before me like a teacher expecting an answer to her question while I chewed on my lip and twisted my pencil, one eye on her, the other on the floor.

This horrible deed of mine occurred about a year earlier. So heinous was the act that I would not confess it, nor even mention it, for fifteen years. On that dark day a year prior, I returned home from school and found that my new pets, two rambunctious gerbils, had become parents of eight pink, peanut-sized babies. Within months these gerbils had hair—and sex drives. Soon their cage was more crowded than the candy line at the neighborhood delicatessen minutes after school let out.

My parents said that I had to get rid of all but two of the gerbils. But I was unable to sell or even give them away. And I was too afraid to let them run free at Rapid Run Park. The pocket guide *How to Raise Gerbils for Fun and Profit* had warned me that gerbils let loose in the wild could survive, multiply, and take over a neighborhood.

I had no choice but to kill them. But how?

Flushing them down the toilet was too risky. The drain may back up and overflow with bilge water and bloated gerbils the size of footballs. Smashing them with a brick was simply too gruesome. So I opted for a cleaner, neater form of gerbilcide: suffocation.

I dropped, one by one, the fifteen animals into a plastic bread bag and twisted the top shut. To ensure that they wouldn't gnaw through the thin resin, I placed their shared body bag in a clear plastic ice cream container. I turned my head and snapped the lid shut. Then, without looking at their cute little noses, I shoved the container to the bottom of an aluminum trashcan underneath our back porch.

That night, I announced to my parents that a boy at school had agreed to take all but the two gerbils that remained in the cage upstairs in the large attic bedroom I shared with my siblings. The two surviving gerbils, both male, seemed overjoyed with their now spacious spread. The thought helped soothe my conscience. And my broken heart.

Disrespect for Mom and Dad, stealing, and a multiple homicide. I was blowing through the Ten Commandments faster than you could say "Saint William, pray for us!" No wonder Satan chose me for his skullduggery.

I snapped out of my daydreaming during the Mass of Satan's Visit when I heard Father Kennedy say, "The Mass has ended. Now go in peace." I thought to myself, *The Mass has ended. Now go to hell.*

As our homeroom teachers shooed us out of church and back to school, I did all I could to hide my panic. Demonic possession was real. In church we heard about Jesus casting out demons. It sometimes seemed that that's all he did besides giving the Apostles a hard time.

But the most convincing evidence of Satan's existence was the wildly popular movie *The Exorcist*, which made its debut the year before. It was based on a true story we were told. Though I hadn't seen the R-rated flick, I heard all the details. Furniture levitating. Heads spinning. The possessed girl puking greenish bile. Sam Flint said that when his parents returned from seeing *The Exorcist* weird things happened in their bedroom, too. He heard strange moans and groans. And the sound of furniture banging against the wall.

My stomach felt queasy as I trudged out of the pew and toward the door with the rest of my class. That day would forever change things. I would divide my life in two parts: BD and AD. Before Devil and After Devil.

I had nowhere to turn.

My beloved church was no longer a sanctuary. And I was too old to sleep with Mom and Dad, though I very much wanted to slip in between them that night and let this private storm blow through in the night.

As I stepped out of the church, squinting in the bright light, I dipped my right hand into the holy water dish and crossed myself, slowly and deliberately.

For several weeks I had trouble concentrating. Even when I scored an A on a test, it didn't quite feel the same. But I tried not to let on. The last thing I needed now was to be the focus of attention. Rather, I needed time to figure this one out. And, like many of the great scientists, I'd have to go at it alone.

I couldn't approach a teacher, parent, or priest. For starters, how could I mention demonic possession without then having to come clean about the candy bars, the gunpowder, and the murdered gerbils? Not to mention all of my lies.

I also feared being disowned by my family and church. Once aware of my possession, my parents or pastor couldn't run the risk of tainting the rest of the family or flock. They'd have no choice but to ship me off to some institution with padded rooms and rusty restraints.

Telling friends was also out of the question. They would either laugh in disbelief or, worse, believe every word and back away in fear. Other kids had been ignored for a week or more just for having feet deemed too big. Or for wearing what someone called a "queer shirt" (even though we didn't know what *queer* meant). To be pinned with possession was a sure social death sentence; not even Lenny Flesch, whose nose constantly oozed a lime-green mucus, would want to hang around me.

A few more weeks passed before Satan came again. This time he jumped me during gym class. The dodgeballs turned to pizzas and the basketball backboards turned to razors. I wanted to move, but I couldn't. I was frozen in place. Fortunately, that wasn't unusual for me in gym. I mostly stood around anyway.

I fought back tears. If I started crying, I risked turning into a sobbing mess of a boy on his hands and knees confessing his sins, something very unbecoming for a Catholic. That kind of crazy behavior was strictly for Protestants. Besides, I had cried a couple of times in class during the preceding few years, once when someone opened up my lunchbox and poured out the chocolate milk in my thermos. I was already teetering on sissy-hood. Any more tears shed and I would only be playing with the girls.

I remained silent, in part, because I was convinced there had to be a cure of some sort. And one occurred to me in the same place that the diagnosis did: St. William's Church. This time, a visiting priest mentioned the Devil, reminding us that the word "evil" was four-fifths of his name. But thankfully, he said, we had in Jesus a friend who could rid the world of the Devil. We just had to pray hard enough, study hard enough, and do enough good deeds.

But, of course! Jesus was my friend, too. He would help purge me of Beelzebub. The obviousness of the cure hit me as hard as the diagnosis. How could I be so thickheaded? The fear and stress were clearly clouding my judgement.

"When Jesus is your true friend, you have no enemies," I recalled Sister Lucy saying. So I decided to do everything within my power to make Jesus a friend, a close one, like the kind you invite to a Friday night sleepover and then, before going to sleep almost sick from too much pop and pretzels, discussing the specs of the perfect tree house: a wooden- *and* a rope-ladder entrance; a platform for heaving water balloons on unsuspecting passersby; and a sign that says, "No girls allowed."

My first step toward cozying up to Jesus was to become an altar boy.

Chapter 3

Brown-Nosing Jesus

> Life was often, if not usually, like this. For
> every good form or expression of something,
> such as saints' bones, there was a bad one, the
> bones of some crazed, blood-thirsty creep. For
> every red-and-white candy mint, one of those
> nasty butterscotch-flavored ones.

I had always envied the altar boys. Their black cassocks, overlaid with the well-starched, bright white surplices, made them seem like mini-priests. Besides, altar boys, or "servers," had ringside seats. They were closer to the action—and to God. Right where I had to be. A position near the priests, the chalices, and the Blessed Hosts would enhance my standing with the Lord.

I signed up with a dozen or so boys for the program. In those days, girls were deemed unworthy of serving; this made good sense to me at the time. Since girls couldn't be priests, why get them started?

We servers-in-training met after school a couple of days for two weeks, each of us mentored by veteran altar boys from the eighth grade. We rehearsed the various positions and duties for the four-altar-boy-Mass (Sundays and holy days) as well as the two-altar-boy-Mass (weekdays, Saturdays, weddings, and funerals). We were also given tours of the sacristy, the area behind the altar where the priests and servers don their vestments and prepare the gadgets and such required for Mass: a chalice, miniature towels embroidered with crosses, the unblessed hosts, and, of course, the wine and water.

The sacristy had some really cool stuff. There was a special sink for pouring out holy water. The pipe went straight into the ground so holy water or bits of blessed hosts would not have to mix with sewer water. "The pipe goes all the way to China," my mentor told me.

The sacristy also had a large walk-in vault, which was where the valuable chalices and crystal were kept. I wished I had something like it at home where I could keep my rockets, chemistry set, and other treasures without fear of my parents or siblings messing with them.

Near the sacristy, one could also look at the relics, the tiny pieces of saints' bone or clothing (or something that *touched* the saints' bone or clothing). Among the relics stored at St. William were those of St. Agnes, St. Cecilia, St. Francis, and, of course, the church's namesake. The minuscule relics were kept in small pendants dressed up with tiny ceramic flowers. These pendants, in turn, were displayed in large, ornate frames.

I always imagined these good "blessed bones" as the polar opposite of the Bloody Bones whom I talked about in my scary storytelling sessions. Life was often, if not usually, like this. For every good form or expression of something, such as saints' bones, there was a bad one, the bones of some crazed, blood-thirsty creep. For every red-and-white candy mint, one of those nasty butterscotch-flavored ones.

17

We servers-in-training had to pay careful attention, for we would wear cassock and surplice only after passing a written test on altar boy terminology and choreography. Distracted by more pretest anxiety than usual, I squeaked by with a seventy-five percent. But it was no surprise. No test had more at stake. After all, my ability to cleanse my soul and escape the Devil's grasp would be difficult, perhaps impossible, without the purification that serving Mass would bring.

My parents, especially my father, had encouraged me to become a server. Dad even offered me a twenty-dollar reward. This surprised me somewhat, because neither Mom nor Dad was the churchgoing type. Both were raised Catholic but had "fallen away." This made it sound as if they didn't have a choice in the matter. And, in a way, perhaps they didn't.

As I would come to understand years later, Mom and Dad were two of countless spiritual casualties when, as a result of Vatican II in the early sixties, the two-thousand-year-old Catholic Church changed dramatically—and virtually overnight. Many faithful were left frustrated, confused, and angry. Mom and Dad still had a place in their hearts for the church, I could tell. They talked lovingly of the old days, especially when the Mass was said in Latin. I didn't quite get it, though. The Mass was incomprehensible as it was. Sitting through it in Latin sounded like torture.

Despite my parents' inactive status, they were committed enough to Catholicism to pay for their kids to attend private school. This was no small sacrifice, given Dad's modest income as a real estate tax appraiser and Mom's part-time gig at a nearby beauty shop. They also demanded that my brothers, sister, and I attend Mass every Sunday.

Often, when the weather was perfect for outside play or too nasty for a comfortable walk to church, I'd protest.

"Why do *we* have to go?" I'd ask, standing at my parents' bedroom door.

"Because the church says you have to," Mom would answer, turning over in bed.

"But *you* don't go," I'd say, cracking the door open a bit more, hoping the light would disturb their sleep.

"That's because we're older."

"What's that have to do with it?"

"You'll understand when you're older."

"But we don't want to go."

"You *have* to. When you turn eighteen you can decide not to go," Mom would say, readjusting her pillow, Dad asking me to shut the door.

I would then share the bad news with my siblings, and we would traipse to church dreaming about just how grand life would be when we turned eighteen. We could skip Mass on sunny days and do whatever else we wanted. Oh, how we hungered for the freedom and easy living of adulthood.

But once at church I didn't mind being there. I always felt better for having gone. Part of it was the calming effect the Mass had on me and, I assumed, everyone. Part of it was the absence of guilt. "God gives you a week, surely you can give him an hour." I heard that countless times from virtually every priest, nun, and seminarian I had ever encountered.

My parents did, however, attend all the big Masses, our First Communions and such. So they were among the thirty people in the pews one Saturday morning at six-thirty when I served my first Mass.

The rookies were always assigned the early morning Masses. But I didn't mind. The smaller crowds meant less embarrassment if I made some horrible mistake, like ringing the bell too early when the priest raised the Host and said, "Do this in remembrance of me." Besides, the extra sacrifice required of the early rise would mean more points from Jesus. And send a signal to Satan. Even before the sun was up, I was devoting my life to the Light of the World. Take that!

I realized during my first ringside Mass that I could enhance the show by keeping a sincere look on my face, my head bowed slightly, and my hands pressed together flat, pointing heavenward. I would be a model server, I decided, a living, breathing, moving altar artifact.

The only flaw in my first Mass was incorrectly handing the priest a cruet, a small, glass pitcher for holding wine and water. I assumed that God knocked off a tenth of a point just like a gymnastics judge docking Olga Korbut for a small slip on the balance beam.

After the Mass, in celebration of my new standing within the church, my family went out to Frisch's Big Boy for breakfast, a rare treat. The Host may have filled our souls, but it didn't quite compare to a tall stack of pancakes. Fulfilling his promise, Dad handed me a twenty-dollar bill when he dipped into his wallet to pay the check. In my world, there were no denominations greater than twenties, and I rarely saw one of those. Twenty bucks meant a dozen rocket motors. Being good definitely had its privileges.

Ready for launch at Rapid Run Park with a rocket I made from a paper towel roll.

The other financial benefit to serving was that the best man in a wedding usually slipped you a buck or two after the ceremony. We altar boys would shove the money in our pockets and then dash outside to be sure we caught a glimpse of the wedding party's parade en route to the reception hall. When the honking, paper streamer-decorated cars passed us on the street, it was custom in our neighborhood to shout "suckers!" at the bride and groom. In return, the wedding party tossed lollipops from their cars.

I was certain that my serving and my other good works would rid me of Satan and ultimately take me to the big pancake breakfast or wedding reception in the sky, the land of milk and honey where syrup and butter, cake and lollipops runneth over.

I couldn't have been more wrong.

Chapter 4

Parental Pleasures

In those early days of jogging, before mall

chain stores offered every imaginable type

and color of sneaker and warm-up suit, Dad

ran in dress slacks and mail-ordered running

shoes. At that point, people assumed that a

grown man running down the street was

either chasing a bus or evading the law.

It occurred to me one day that if I took the first initial from each of the names my parents gave their three sons, oldest to youngest, it spelled LSD, the popular drug of the day. "You think you're just experimenting," teachers would warm us, "but then you get hooked and end up going to prison for stealing TV sets to feed your addiction."

I thought this **Larry Steve Dave** name choice might be a sign. Of what, I wasn't exactly sure, since Mom and Dad weren't the drug-taking types. Though Mom told me that she must have been high on something to drop out of school and have babies. "It's called being high on love," Dad would say in return.

I envied friends for having parents who looked and acted more like parents should. Greg Teal's father had gray hair and smoked a pipe. His dignified manner impressed me. Lou Bella's mother never wore gym shoes and she occasionally had ladies over for card parties. Her attention to womanly detail seemed most

Mom and Dad a month before my birth.

admirable. Kevin Craine's father coached football and drove a station wagon with paneling on the side. His appreciation for fatherly standards was awe-inspiring.

My mom and dad acted more like, well, kids. Something that's not surprising to me now, nearing forty, as I consider that Mom and Dad were barely over thirty-years-old at this time. My parents' youth and spunk, I could tell, intrigued my friends.

Mom was thin with expressive eyes that, like the statues in church, always seemed to be trained on you regardless of the angle from which you looked back. Well into adulthood, some of my childhood friends confessed that they thought my mom was, in the lingo of our youth, a "fox."

Mom always appeared on the verge of laughing. A constant teaser, she often showed a photo of my brother Dave, just hours after he was born. His head was so coned-shaped he looked like you could turn him over and dig fence post holes. Mom convinced Dave, an energetic, cute kid with light brown hair, that his head was so deformed at birth that doctors were forced to perform a transplant. It was never clear whose shapely head now sat on Dave's shoulders. Mom said if she knew, she would tell us. But the doctors refused to divulge the donor. Hospital policy.

Mom and Dad liked to jump rope, walk around the neighborhood, and otherwise stay on the go. They even enjoyed popular music. Dad was especially fond of "The Cover of the Rolling Stone" by Dr. Hook and the Medicine Show. Mom's Carole King *Tapestry* album was a favorite of hers—and mine. Our little stereo stood always ready for Carole, Three Dog Night, Neil Diamond, Gordon Lightfoot, and Kenny Rogers and the First Edition.

Dad was of average height, strong, yet thin. His arms were nearly covered in freckles, which seemed appropriate given his childlike demeanor.

Once my friend Greg Teal spent the night, and Dad encouraged us to build a haunted house in my bedroom. When Greg and I were done, Dad said he would volunteer to be our first victim. This amazed and impressed Greg. Haunted house building wasn't the kind of thing his pipe-smoking father would have ever proposed, let alone participated in.

Greg, a husky kid in love with anything fried or grease-covered, sat down on my bed as we thoughtfully discussed our house of horrors.

"Let's hang a sheet here and one there, so we have four chambers," I suggested, pointing around the room like the foreman on a construction site.

"That's hip," Greg said. "We'll lay your Invisible Man model on the nightstand like somebody's operating on him."

"Yeah! And let's pour ketchup on him," I said, my face scrunched, mimicking the look I expected Dad to give the fake blood.

"Cool! And let's hang that GI Joe doll by his feet from your bedpost."

"What about the third chamber?" I asked. "How about hanging my rubber snakes there? And let's open a jar of my dad's limburger cheese so it smells like dead, rotting bodies."

"Neat-oh!" Greg said, his tongue sticking out the side of his mouth. I could practically see his mind working overtime.

"I'll lie underneath a blanket like I'm in a coffin. When my dad comes through, I'll jump out."

"Put some red pen marks on your neck like you were sucked by a vampire."

"Great idea."

"And I'll flip the lights on and off like lightning," Greg said, nearly foaming at the mouth.

After we carefully constructed our bedroom of bedlam, Dad toured the tight chambers, crawling around on his stomach, feigning fright. Just as Greg had promised, he flicked the lights to simulate lightning, while I groaned the groans of an irate monster unable to break free of his dungeon chains. Dad was impressed. He thought we might have a future in haunted house or Hollywood set design.

For some reason, playing around with devilish stuff like fake blood and rubber snakes didn't bother me. I suppose I knew it was just for fun, like Halloween. It paid no real respect to evil but rather "teased" it, so Jesus wouldn't mind.

But the Devil seemed to take notice. He continued to visit whenever he felt like it, turning people and things I knew well into other people and things. I'd hear something, but could never tell exactly what it was. Could it be Satan trying to speak directly to me? Asking *me* to do something? If so, did I *really* want to hear? I didn't think so.

The Devil would leave as quickly as he came. His visits lasted only a short while, often just seconds. But they seemed to go on for hours, as if I went to sleep for a long while, dreamed the night away, and woke up at the exact moment of time that I dozed off. And Satan always left me with an odd feeling, like when you wake up in the middle of a dream and it takes a second or two to figure out who and where you are. Or like when you hang upside down on the jungle gym until there's so much blood in your head that you barely remember your name.

The chaos in my head rocked me to my core, but I managed to tell no one. Not a single soul. Not even my parents. What could they, or anyone for that matter, do about it? I worried, too, that telling someone would only anger Satan and invite more trouble, sort of like telling a teacher that one of the eighth graders is harassing you. It only seemed to make the bully all the more eager to catch you alone on the way home from school.

I was not about to be Satan's snitch.

Besides being a homemade haunted house aficionado, Dad was also a long-distance runner. He was among the first wave of people to embrace running as a means of staying in shape. He was jogging before Frank Shorter, the 1972 Olympic marathon champion, helped launch the running boom that still echoes today.

In those early days of jogging, before mall chain stores offered every imaginable type and color of sneaker and warm-up suit, Dad ran in dress slacks and mail-ordered running shoes. At that point, people assumed that a grown man running down the street was either chasing a bus or evading the law. Dad also participated in some road races well before they, too, became common weekend fare.

On race days, the family would pile into our tan VW bug, which we dubbed the "Beige Bomber." My siblings and I would fight over who got to sit in the cubbyhole behind the rear seat and above the rear-mounted engine, which seemed to give everything it had every time it had to get us somewhere.

Dad was seldom, if ever, a contender to win the road races, but he held his own, beating most. While Dad and his fellow competitors ran races of typically two to ten miles out in the country, Mom would read a magazine, and we kids would explore the nearby farm fields and railroad tracks. I wondered where the rails led and dreamed of far-off places like the Grand Canyon and Yellowstone, places well beyond our family's income—and the Beige Bomber's range.

In addition to his running, Dad pedaled his ten-speed bike, then also a rarity, around town. All the biking and running aggravated Dad's chronic back pain. He employed two primary means of relief. The first was having one of his kids rub or walk on his back. Often this was just considered one of our weekly chores, like taking out the garbage. But when he was feeling particularly generous, he would pay as much as a dime a minute. That was enough to turn five minutes of stomping or pushing into a Coke and a candy bar.

Dad's second method of back pain relief was a special device that hung from the top of a door. Dad would sit on a chair, a cloth mask wrapped around his forehead and under his chin. Attached to the mask were ropes that ran up over pulleys and then down to a suspended cloth sack. Inside it, Dad usually put a brick or a five-pound bag of sugar to apply soothing pressure to his spine. On days when Mom was less than pleased with Dad, she would threaten to toss a bowling ball or a twenty-pound frozen turkey into the sack. Either would have snapped Dad's neck.

A big believer in the healing powers of a proper diet, Dad devoured the advice in health food books and magazines such as *Prevention*. One of his cure-alls was wheat germ. He put it atop foods of every sort. We had great fun teasing Dad about his dietary idiosyncrasies, especially since health food guru Euell Gibbons starred in television commercials for a breakfast cereal.

"Ever eat a pine tree?" he'd ask at the beginning of the ad. So whenever we saw Dad with a mouthful of health food, we'd ask, "Ever eat a pine tree?" He would answer, "Only after I sprinkle some wheat germ on it."

Dad also had a juicer. I loved it when he made apple juice, because the sweet, fragrant liquid tasted better than anything store-bought. It was as if you could taste the leaves and the bark, too. But Dad usually made carrot juice, the thick, syrupy stuff I wouldn't even try. Dad not only swallowed it without wincing, he actually seemed to enjoy it. Mom teased that he would turn orange.

About the only thing Dad seemed to enjoy drinking as much as carrot juice was beer. Like Whoopee Cushions and plastic statues of the Blessed Virgin, beer was omnipresent in my world. Cincinnati, a town with a rich German heritage, once had dozens of breweries. I couldn't recall a birthday, a backyard picnic, or gathering of any sort at which beer wasn't served. The beer booths were always among the most popular—and profitable—at the parish festivals. There were even beer taps in St. William's undercroft, the church basement that served as a bingo and party hall.

Dad never drank liquor, just beer, and only after a day of work, a five-mile run, and perhaps the most strenuous part of all: Mom's dinner. Dad did most of his drinking at home, except when he visited a family member's home or, as was the case on most Saturday nights, at his favorite watering hole, a bar named Dase's Place.

Drinking changed Dad, often in a flash. He could be crawling through a haunted house one minute, all smiles and fake grunts, and just a few minutes later he could be ranting and raving like a maniac created in a deranged scientist's lab, his speech punctuated with dirty words. It was usually something significant that set Dad off, like leaving a bike in the driveway or pouring so much cereal into your bowl that it overflowed onto the table. He once blamed a bad race he had on his kids' poor behavior. I wasn't a runner, but it seemed like a big fat excuse to me. But I didn't tell him that, of course.

He was a great dad and a happy person most of the time. It's why his outbursts had an eerie dimension to them, as if something had control of his mind, too. I wondered if his drinking and my demonic possession might be connected somehow. Each was highly unpredictable, confusing, and hurtful.

I responded to Satan's visits and Dad's fits much the same way: I remained still and quiet until the episode passed. My focus on good behavior was a means of not only distancing myself from the Devil but also providing as few excuses as reasonably possible to give Dad, or anyone for that matter, a reason to blow up.

I attributed Dad's short temper to some sort of character flaw—in myself. Lord knows that I wasn't perfect. I had many weaknesses and shortcomings. This much I knew, now more than ever with Satan chasing me.

Chapter 5

A Sporting Chance

> I imagined the eucharistic wafers weakening
> the demon inside me in much the same way
> that kryptonite crippled Superman. Though I
> was gorging myself on God's flesh, I needed to
> do more.

By the end of fifth grade I had suffered through dozens of visits by the Devil. One occurred during recess. For a few moments I was standing in the midst of the strangest collection of people: my Grandpa Elmer, Einstein, and a Vietnam War soldier. Turtles and nails, rather than footballs and softballs, soared through the air. It was like watching a movie, say *Brian's Song*, and all of sudden the actors are replaced with characters from other movies. Out goes Brian Piccolo as portrayed by James Caan and in comes Brian Piccolo as portrayed by The Professor on *Gilligan's Island*. This sort of colorful, arguably comic imagery might seem kind of neat and even interesting, but it never, ever *felt* that way. I suppose because it was forced upon me. A cherry sucker tastes good, but not when one is shoved down your throat. That happened to me once when I dove onto my bed, forgetting I had a sucker in my mouth.

The Devil wasn't about to let me have any fun. If he was willing to visit during Mass, why should he have any qualms interrupting a game of schoolyard catchers? He even had the gall to drop by while I sat at attention in Sister Patricia's math class.

Tall and thin, with gray hair always perfectly coiffed, Sister Patricia had no patience for classroom shenanigans, dirty fingernails, or, worse, forgetting to reduce your fractions to their least common denominator. Her deep love of Jesus and her willingness to confront any troublemaker should have been enough to convince Lucifer to wait for me until after class. But it wasn't.

While Sister Patricia paced the aisles and we suffered through word problems, Satan came to visit. I was certain Sister would sense that her archenemy had infiltrated her classroom, that she would smell his presence, and—out of love for me, her Christian brother—slap us both around.

This time during the demonic dementia Lisa Riley became my mom; Ralph Klunk, Henry Kissinger; Mary Kesterman, the Joker from TV's *Batman*. The voices seemed almost to be taunting me now. Satan came and went faster than I could finish even one pesky word problem about a grocer separating apples and oranges.

Sister Patricia didn't notice a thing. A very bad sign, indeed.

Fortunately, my soul-purifying plan was well underway. Hardly a week went by without me serving several Masses. These, combined with Sunday Mass and the mandatory weekly class Mass, meant that I was consuming the Blessed Host—what we Catholics believe to be the *actual* body of Jesus—about five times a week.

"You are what you eat," Dad would say right before swallowing his stinky vitamins with a carrot juice chaser, flexing his muscles like Jack La Lanne. No doubt eating God's flesh would help me flex my spiritual muscle. I imagined the eucharistic wafers weakening the demon inside me in much the same way that kryptonite crippled Superman. Though I was gorging myself on God's flesh, I needed to do more.

I sat down one day with pencil and paper to evaluate my overall condition against the three basic people "parts" that Sister Lucy said we all had: spirit, mind, and body. My soul was becoming more wholesome, thanks to all that serving, praying, and Communion chomping. Not to mention countless good deeds. I placed a check mark next to "spirit."

My report cards were mostly A's and B's. One teacher even wrote that I was "a joy" to have in class. I placed a checkmark next to "mind." Things were looking good.

Then I got to "body," which left a lot to be desired. I was always among the last to be picked when teams were chosen for recess football and softball games. I had to do something about this. But what? I had not a single athletic bone in my body. In my one and only peewee football season I saw maybe forty-five seconds of total play, if you count the time spent running on and off the field to the line of scrimmage. Mom and Dad came to every game, even though there wasn't much of me to watch.

My team won the league championship, which meant that I came home with a small trophy. I displayed it proudly in my room. A few days later, after drinking a few beers, Dad got pissed at something and told me that the water boy was more deserving of the trophy. Dad was right. I couldn't claim any responsibility for the team's success. Ashamed, I hid the trophy in a drawer. But I couldn't forget that it was there, nor what Dad had said to me. A couple of days later, I tossed the trophy away.

My attempt at playing baseball met with even greater humiliation. During the final game of the season, the coach—out of pity or in need of entertainment—put me at first base. I walked to the position like a man being led to his last meal, one he didn't even get to choose. Deep left field would have been just fine by me.

When the first batter approached the plate, I prayed that he would walk, strikeout, or pop up to the catcher. My pleas went unanswered. The batter hit a grounder and made it safely to first, though thankfully the ball never made it to me. I then focused intently on the next batter, as if through my stare I could will a strikeout or, better still, a homer hit so deep into the weeds the ball would never be found.

Lost in a trance, I didn't realize that the runner on first had taken an enormous lead off. The pitcher, however, did. He turned around and whizzed a fastball at me. I caught it perfectly. With my right temple. I fell on the ground and cried, coaches and teammates rushing to my aid.

Without doing something to improve my physical fitness, I risked toppling the three-legged stool upon which I would stand and reach for God's hand. For several weeks, I contemplated the critical deficiency on my evaluation sheet: no checkmark next to "body."

The answer to my completing the trifecta came via a school announcement about the formation of a track team. Once again the answer was right in front of me. Certainly, or at least probably, I could run like Dad. And I need not worry about throwing something. Or having something thrown at me. Perfect.

Joining the track team would also raise my stature with Dad. He would be tickled to see me taking up his sport of choice. He was always complaining that track and field didn't get enough airtime on *Wide World of Sports*. Dad thought Jim McKay had a bias toward rodeo, demolition derby, and cliff diving. Dad wanted to see more of his track heroes, guys such as Jim Ryun, the first high school athlete to run a mile in less than four minutes. Of course God would also be happy to see me on the team. "Strong bodies please the Lord," Sister Lucy said. It was time for me to rebuild the temple that was my body.

At lunch I discussed the track team with Kevin Craine, another multiple sport reject, whose nose twitched whenever he got nervous. "You going to try out for track?" I asked through a mouthful of macaroni.

"Sure, I hear they won't cut anybody."

"The coaches may change their mind when they see us," I said.

"You're real funny."

"I have to be 'cause I ain't pretty like you," I said, tossing my head back and forth, flipping my hair with my hand. "What event you trying out for?"

"I prefer the field events," Kevin said, lifting half a peanut-butter-and-jelly sandwich to his shoulder as if preparing to heave a shot put.

"Vickie Norton would be better at it than you," I said, nodding toward her, two tables over.

"But we'd need a truck to get her four hundred pounds to the meet," Kevin noted, adding about 250 pounds to the truth. "Maybe I'll try the pole vault."

"The pole vault! You get weak in the knees when you stand on a chair," I said.

"I'll do it with my eyes shut."

"You can't, dork. You'll end up with pole up your butt."

Breaking a pretzel rod in half, Kevin said, "You're real funny."

"I have to be 'cause I ain't pretty like you," I said again, framing my face with my hands.

"Funny," he said, shaking his broken pretzel rod at me. "You going to run distances just like your old man?"

"I suppose so."

Kevin and I reported for track practice the following day. Our coach, Tom Norton, was a clean-cut, friendly junior from Archbishop Elder High, the all-boys school that Kevin and I would attend after graduating from St. William. Coach Norton had run a season or two with Elder's track team. So he knew what he was talking about. He even had a stopwatch around his neck.

With clipboard in hand and the team at his feet, Coach Norton shared some bad news. First, most of the season, in fact, virtually *all* of the season, was over, but the championship meet for which we had only a week to train. Second, we didn't have enough recruits to field a junior and senior team. Instead, everyone, including us fifth graders, would race in the senior division with seventh and eighth graders.

The news didn't ruin my enthusiasm. Track wasn't like baseball, football, or basketball. There were no complex rules to grasp, no positions to master, and no plays to memorize. It's just one foot in front of the other. I could probably manage that much.

Coach Norton divided us into sprinters and long-distance runners. My thin frame and my father's running reputation put me speedily in the long-distance camp. This was good. The only place I had fast-twitch muscle fibers was in my eyelids.

Kevin ended up in the distance running group, too. He told the coach that fast running aggravated his asthma, a condition I didn't even know he had (though he did seem to breathe more heavily around Gayle Morris).

The team practiced three times before the championship meet. After some windmills, toe touches, and other calisthenics, the sprinters ran 50- and 100-yard dashes on St. William's asphalt playground. We long-distance runners jogged and mostly walked around the block several times covering what I now would guess to be about a mile.

With other sports it became clear from the first swing of the bat, the first free throw, the first movement off the line of scrimmage that I had the athletic prowess of Jerry Lewis. But with running it was different.

35

Those familiar with my sports history may have expected me to trip and fall down, maybe even run backward when I was supposed to run forward. But, no. I could run. By this I don't mean to suggest that I demonstrated some unusually rare aptitude for the sport, but merely that I could run without hurting myself or causing my coaches and teammates to shake their heads in disgust.

Our team showed up for the Catholic schools championship meet in cut-off shorts and T-shirts of every color. One kid even wore his black dress shoes because, he said, the heels would give him extra traction. Our inconsistent, shabby look conflicted with our school's official mascot: a bespectacled, top-hatted robber baron. It never made much sense to me: a working-class parish represented by a wealthy businessman. Besides, barons just don't intimidate the way, say, an eagle with exposed, blood-stained claws does.

Virtually all of the other teams wore silky, shiny uniforms, their school names emblazoned across their chests. They looked notably stronger and faster. These were kids from the better-off parishes. They were the ones who lived in homes with paneled basements where ping-pong and pool tables stood ever ready to play. They were the ones with garbage disposals, which, I had heard, made their wastewater so rich in nutrients that rats the size of cars were sometimes found in their sewers. They were the ones whose summer vacations included trips to national parks and sandy beaches.

As if the flashy, fast-looking uniforms weren't unfair advantage enough, one parish even had the perfect name to wear into battle: Our Lady of Victory. Unbeatable.

"I feel stupid," Kevin said, standing next to the concession stand in his cut-off brown corduroy shorts and red T-shirt, sipping a Coke.

"The STP logo on your shirt makes you look fast," I said, trying to console him. Truth was, I felt stupid, too, in my denim shorts and one of Dad's sweat-stained T-shirts. I thought it would make other competitors think that I had been working out all year.

"But their uniforms are so cool," Kevin said, his nose twitching like a rabbit's.

"But we look meaner and rougher," I replied.

"No, we just look stupider and poorer."

"It's not what you wear, but how fast you run," I said. My dad said the guy who won the Olympic marathon in 1960 didn't wear shoes."

"Maybe so. But I bet he had a uniform."

"Shut up and stretch out."

Kevin finished last in the first heat for the 880-yard run, a half-mile. He ran faster than I ever saw him run—for about fifty yards. Ultimately, his pencil-thin, fifth-grade legs were no match for those of powerful eighth graders, especially those jutting out of shiny running shorts.

My event, the two-mile relay, was the last of the day. Each of the four runners would cover two laps of the quarter-mile cinder track. I seemed puny in the group of seventh and eighth graders when huddled at the start line for the referee's instructions. We were reminded that we had to hand—not toss—the baton from runner to runner. Dropping the baton meant automatic disqualification.

The starter's gun went off at about dusk. Our few days of training turned out to be at least a few too few. We were left in the dust from the first turn, eventually lapped—and then lapped yet again.

I ran the third leg. When Pete Fritsch handed me the baton, I initially pounded the cinder track too fast, a common mistake among first-timers. I did eventually settle into a rhythm, though.

37

Mom and Dad were on the track's edge urging me on. Dad waved his stopwatch above his head, reminding me that time was passing by. Not fast enough, I thought. My thighs and lungs burned. The only thing that hurt worse was my right hand. For fear of dropping the baton—something that I seemed predestined to do—I kept a GI Joe kung fu grip on it. My fist turned to rock. But I managed to make it around the track twice without losing too much ground.

Pat Callahan, our final and best runner, yanked the baton out of my hand. But by then some teams had almost finished. Even the great Jim Ryun couldn't have helped. The meet organizers were turning off the stadium lights before Pat had crossed the finish line.

"Look on the bright side," Kevin said. "People won't see us lose."

Earlier in the meet, one of the eighth graders on our team managed a seventh-place finish in the long jump to earn our team its one and only point. Our Lady of Victory did well, of course. We were beat nearly as badly as a team could be. Kevin said our team wasn't even qualified to compete in the Special Olympics. We vowed revenge the following year.

I didn't fully share in the team's sense of disappointment, though. For once, I made a contribution. Pitiful perhaps, but a contribution nonetheless. I didn't watch from the bench. I didn't make my teammates and coaches snicker. More to the point, I didn't fear being in the game. I felt better about this failure than I had about any of my other teams' victories.

Immediately after the race, I began anticipating the next track and field season. I was so relieved to have found a sport that fit me. That night, a proud veteran of a week of training and a championship meet, I retrieved the paper on which I evaluated myself. Next to "body" I placed a check mark.

I was on the right path, doing things to strengthen every part of me: body, mind, and most importantly, spirit. But did I have the endurance to stay on the path of goodness for as long as I had to? Or would the Prince of Darkness just turn the lights off on me?

Chapter 6

Heavy Artillery

> Even outside the religious realm, there was
> room for magic and mystery. I was a believer.
> How could I not be? I had exploited such
> powers and changed the course of human
> history—in smoky bingo parlors and on the
> bloody battlefields of Vietnam.

The Devil's visits continued. Always unannounced. Always sudden. Always upsetting. I had grown accustomed to people asking after episodes if I was OK. "You seemed distracted," they would say. I had become quite adept at reassuring friends and family members alike that everything was cool, that there was absolutely nothing to worry about, that I was fine and dandy. I had a pocketful of pat responses: "Just thinking about the homework assignment," "I got to bed late last night," and, my favorite, "My grandma's real sick." I learned early that when you're quick with an excuse, people usually accept it without question.

The fact that Satan could overtake my mind and influence events was not a difficult concept to embrace. There was most certainly a spirit world populated by angels and demons. We heard about them in church and religion class. Angels helped beam heavenly powers down to the religious medals many of us wore. And if we died with one around our necks, we were guaranteed more leniency when St. Peter met us at the Pearly Gates. The medal was something of a backstage pass.

Pleas to saints, we were told, often paid dividends, too. For example, if you lost something, a prayer to St. Anthony would substantially increase your odds of finding it.

The spirit world also included guardian angels, the winged, ghostlike beings who kept an eye out for us. Credit was heaped on guardian angels for all sorts of assists and "saves."

My paternal Grandma Marge once looked downward while shopping and found a ten-dollar bill. She gave the credit to her guardian angel. Her sister, my Great Aunt Lena, thanked her guardian angel for making her sneeze once at just the right second. This heaven-sent nose tickle caused Aunt Lena to miss a step. Had she not paused, she said, she would have walked right into the path of a speeding car.

I assumed that my guardian angel was still in training, had fallen down on the job, or, worse, had moved to the dark side.

Even outside the religious realm, there was room for magic and mystery. I was a believer. How could I not be? I had exploited such powers and changed the course of human history—in smoky bingo parlors and on the bloody battlefields of Vietnam.

I turned the bingo world upside down with the help of a magic rock. Jim Turrell, one of my classmates, had a father who took up stone polishing. Jim would occasionally sell jewelry and decorative items made with his father's polished rocks. Jim did an especially brisk business around Christmastime, when we all needed something special for our parents and grandparents. Nothing said "Happy Holidays" quite like polished rock earrings and toenail clippers.

41

One spring I bought—with stolen money—a key chain to give to my Grandma Marge, the world's greatest, I thought. Short, with traditional Italian features, she looked like she stepped right out of central casting to play the Italian grandmother in some spaghetti commercial. She showered my siblings and cousins with attention, or more specifically, food, toys, and candy money. Grandma Marge's cooking was outstanding, especially her pasta, bread, and cookies. A favorite in the family was her fried bread, what we called "pizza freetz." It was perfect with salami and Swiss cheese.

We grandkids took turns sleeping over at Grandma's on Friday nights. We ate like kings and stayed up late to watch *Love, American Style*, one of Grandma's favorites. In the morning, we would hop a bus and ride downtown to shop, usually grabbing a bite to eat at Woolworth's lunch counter. On the ride home, there would always be a new piece of clothing as well as candy or a small toy on our laps.

We'd get the same treatment on our birthdays. Grandma would give us a package of underwear or tube socks, but always a toy, too. And something we really wanted, like a scale model of a Cro-Magnon man complete with club and saber-toothed tiger. We kids associated all this kindness with Grandma, even though it was her husband, Grandpa Elmer, who, as the breadwinner, made her generosity possible.

Grandpa Elmer was a thin man, always hiking his pants up. He enjoyed beer and playing the ponies. He studied racing forms the way I did the Johnson Smith novelty catalog, marveling at the smart minds behind Silly String and those pens that doubled as telescopes. Among Grandpa's treasures were photos of Man O' War and Secretariat that hung proudly in his home.

Every time I got a report card, I shared it with Grandma first. She would heap praise upon me, put her latest baked creation in front of me, and then pinch my cheeks and call me "one smart cookie." She would also say, "I can't wait to tell the ladies at bingo about all your A's."

For Grandma, bingo was serious business. It was more than the chance to win some cash. It was a social event. And a competition. Between games one grandma would casually note that her granddaughter won her class art competition. Another grandma would respond with a compliment—and then note that her grandson's baseball team won the league championship. Yet another grandma would offer her congratulations—and then announce that her granddaughter was deemed best in her dance class. The boasting was a true bloodsport. And we grandkids were handsomely rewarded any time we supplied our grandmas with ammunition.

After sharing my report cards with Grandma, my belly extended from overdosing on her homemade chocolate chip cookies, I would waddle out of her apartment, a dollar and a pack of *sugarless* gum in my hands. I would sometimes wonder how a boy so loved by a woman so kind and generous as Grandma could also be the target of the Evil One himself? It made less sense than Pet Rocks.

I gave Grandma the polished stone key chain as a means of saying thanks for all her goodness—and scoring more of her affection in its many forms. The key chain's shiny light-brown rock had dark ribbons like those in caramel swirl ice cream. Grandma immediately declared it her good luck charm and took it with her to the weekly bingo sessions at St. William and St. Lawrence, a nearby parish also in Price Hill. She would spin her lucky rock above her cards before each game began.

With rock in hand, Grandma Marge enjoyed a hot streak the likes of which she and her bingo bunch had never seen. She even won 250 dollars on a cover-all. True to form, Grandma always shared a bit of her winnings with me, which I promptly spent on candy, squirt guns, and bags of army soldiers. She even took me to a couple of bingo games, always double-checking my card—after she checked her six—to be sure I didn't miss a number.

The lucky key chain reinforced an important lesson: those who do good deeds reap rewards. After about six months, though, Grandma's luck ebbed and the once lucky stone turned back into just another old rock, albeit a very shiny one. In so doing, it taught yet another lesson: The spirit world is unpredictable, fickle. Easy come, easy go. This wasn't necessarily a bad thing, though. It gave me hope that one day the Devil would just up and go. And leave me alone.

My second impressive feat of wonder made possible by the spirit world occurred several years prior to Grandma's hot streak. This earlier magic of mine brought an end to the Vietnam War, something even we kids had grown sick of. My parents' early marriage and young family probably saved my father from a tour of duty. But we still felt connected to the war, in part because of the TV news and also because Mom wore a POW bracelet.

Around the time when the TV seemed to be filled with war reports interspersed with protest footage, Mom presented me with a chicken wishbone. We each tugged on a half. I won. I wished for an end to the war. I had seen enough craziness on TV, and I wanted desperately for Mom's POW to come home.

The very next day, President Nixon made some remark on TV about a pending end to American involvement in the war. I expected him to thank me by name, but the ungrateful man did not. No wonder he was ultimately kicked out of office.

The true horrors of the war were, of course, beyond my reach. But, a few years later, while still in elementary school, I got a disturbing glimpse thanks to publisher and free-speech advocate Larry Flynt. He was waging a legal battle in Cincinnati over the right to sell his magazine, *Hustler*. Local officials deemed it an affront to public morals. I took this to mean that the naked women in his magazine were really ugly.

To make his point about what is truly obscene, Flynt mailed to thousands of homes in Cincinnati a booklet entitled "War: The Real Obscenity," crammed with color photos of Vietnam War battle scenes. There was so much buzz about the

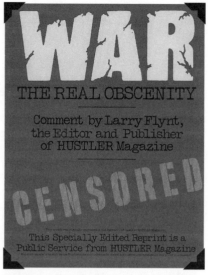

An eye-opening look at the atrocities of war, courtesy of Mr. Larry Flynt, "defender of the first amendment."

publication that if asked, most of us boys would have rather seen the war pictorial than an actual *Hustler*.

"Did you see Larry Flynt's war magazine?" Lou Bella asked me before science class.

"Not yet. I hear it's got some great photos in it," I said, not taking my glance off the dinosaur I was doodling on my school folder.

"Yeah, I can't wait to see them," Lou said, his bushy eyebrows rising to the top of his forehead.

"I'd love to put some up in my bedroom," I remarked, thinking the manly photos would look good next to my Cincinnati Reds pennant, complete with factory-produced autographs of the Big Red Machine, including Pete Rose.

"It'd look cool next to one of your rockets," Lou said.

"Yours would look good near your American flag sticker on your window."

Mom snatched Flynt's pictorial from the mailman before he even had a chance to put it in our mailbox. Mom refused to share it despite my requests, which flew as fast and furious as shrapnel. She said, "not in a million years," and then read in a deep, slow voice, like Walter Cronkite's, the notice printed on the cover: "Warning: Material of an adult nature. This literature is not intended for minors, and under no circumstances are they to view it or possess it."

"C'mon, Mom!" I pleaded.

"Forget it, Stevie." Mom always called me Stevie. (Still does.) So did Grandma. Truth is, I didn't mind.

Fortunately, some other kids managed to get behind parental enemy lines and capture a copy. Rick Stanch, a thickheaded troublemaker with a superb "don't mess with me" walk, flashed the war mag around in gym class when the teacher had to leave for a few moments. I joined a pack of boys under the basketball hoop. We swarmed around Rick for a glimpse of real battle scenes that we had, until then, just imagined or seen on TV in an edited-for-civilians fashion.

We all pushed and shoved to get a better look. At first there was considerable chatter and shouts of "My turn! My turn!" We each elbowed our way to the front. We dared not blink for fear we'd miss something. But the commotion came to a sudden stop, as if what we thought was a brand new toy turned out instead to be a box of maggots. We were stunned, horrified, and troubled all at once.

What I saw on the shiny pages of the magazine was nothing like the neat and orderly images of battle I had imagined. In my fiction, there was some blood, but no real pain, no real suffering—kind of like ketchup on an Invisible Man model in one of my bedroom haunted houses. But Flynt's photos showed men, real men, with limbs blown off, their slimy guts spilling onto the ground, their heads blown apart, their brains oozing out like Jell-O that had gotten too warm. I could hear these men screaming. I could see the horror in their eyes. I could feel the lump in my throat.

Flynt's magazine was more evidence that the Devil did exist. If he didn't, neither would those pictures.

After that day, no one expressed much interest in toying around with plastic army soldiers or playing war after school. It no longer seemed like a fun thing to do.

Back in the fifth grade, I decided to bring out the heavier artillery in my own battle: exorcism. I was aware that the church performed the ritual, but I wasn't about to step forward and request one. I wasn't the most popular kid in class, but I wasn't the least popular either. If word spread that I was a candidate for exorcism, I would fall to the bottom of the rung. Parents and grandparents would instruct their kids and grandkids to stay away from me. And understandably so. Bad luck was known to be contagious. Certainly demonic possession was even more so.

About once a week, when I found myself alone at home with at least ten minutes to spare, I would conduct my own purification ritual. With the curtains drawn and lights turned off, I would place the family Bible on the dining room table. I would open it randomly to some spread in the New Testament, the better, truer, more Catholic part of the Bible, I thought then. To the left of the Good Book I would lay the family crucifix, which usually sat on Dad's dresser.

Above the Bible I would light a small votive candle, one I took from the foot of the Mary statue inside St. William after depositing fifteen cents into the padlocked alms container—a sizeable sacrifice, given that it was the going rate of a candy bar. To the right of the Bible I set an eight-ounce Welch's grape juice bottle filled with holy water, an Easter present from Sister Lucy. I would then place atop the Bible a small piece of factory-made, vitamin-fortified, store-bought Wonder Bread.

To set the proper mood and ready myself, I would drape a black plastic rosary around my neck and perform the sign of the cross. I would genuflect three times, say a "Hail Mary," and then, while on my knees, recite an "Our Father." I would bow three times while kissing the crucifix at the end of my rosary. Finally, I would genuflect three more times.

These spiritual calisthenics were but the prelude to the real exorcism: the blessing and consumption of the Wonder Bread.

To purify the bread and give it demon-fighting powers, I would hold it over the sacred votive candle until slightly singed. I'd then sprinkle a bit of holy water on the crustless morsel. (Crust on Communion just seemed improper.)

I would then hold the Communion up above my bowed head and ask God to bless it and turn it into his body. After swallowing the blessed bread, I would conclude the ceremony by laying my hand on the Bible and saying a final "Our Father," or, if in a hurry, the shorter "Hail Mary." Then I'd rush to get all of the religious stuff back in its proper places before someone came home and caught me in the act.

No wonder I was a nervous kid. I not only had to hide my curse, but also my cure.

Chapter 7

False Gods

I envied those kids whose families worshiped together. Surrounded by such families in church, I felt a bit embarrassed there sans parents. Mine were, at best, lazy, at worst, pagans. In either case, their nonpracticing status wasn't helping me any.

Despite my self-administered exorcisms and other devil-bashing techniques, Lucifer kept visiting. He came to me at school, at the swimming pool, even once on the bus as my friends and I rode downtown to shop at the novelty store for joy buzzers, fake dog doo, and disappearing ink. Hallucinating while moving down the road at thirty miles per hour added a whole new dimension to the experience. The view out of the window was a landscape littered with giant milk bottles, dish rags, and characters from TV shows. The vibrations in the seat from the grinding motor below, combined with the crunching in my head, made my whole body tingle like your foot does when it falls asleep. It was all over in seconds, and by the time we got downtown, my stomach felt a bit upset. The fake vomit didn't seem as funny that day.

The fact that Satan was dropping by more frequently didn't demoralize me. The way I saw it, my condition may have been getting worse, but it would have been careening out of control even faster if I hadn't been walking the path of righteousness. Or at least trying to.

I still folded under certain pressures, the bad escaping through cracks in my character like lava flowing from a fracture in the earth's surface. The result was a regular eruption of naughty behavior. For instance, my loose bicycle chain kept jumping off my sprocket, and each time, though I pledged I wouldn't anymore, I yelled "Goddammit," breaking the Second Commandment, while weaving back and forth down the sidewalk, dragging my gym shoes on the concrete, aiming for a soft patch of grass. (This violation was doubly offensive in that it inevitably caused Mom, when she noticed my grease-stained shirts in the laundry, to break the Second Commandment, too.)

Temptation followed me everywhere, whether I was on my bike or not. A sugar addict, I stole money from my parents and classmates in order to buy pop and candy. With my teeth tingling and my belly gurgling, I realized that ambrosia somehow tasted better when purchased with someone else's money. I hated myself for this. But I couldn't deny it.

I also hurt people's feelings. I told Nick Greene that a rash on his face "looked like a monkey's butt." I called Renee White "a stupid moron." But all my sinful behavior wasn't entirely my fault. No way. In one case, the bright beam of blame could be aimed at TV talk show host Merv Griffin.

Merv was royalty in our house. His show was one of my parents' favorites. Larry, Dave, Teri, and I learned not to bother or irritate our parents in any way when Merv was on the tube interviewing the day's celebs, people such as Eva Gabor, Flip Wilson, Barry Manilow, and one of Dad's favorites: The Amazing Kreskin.

I wasn't typically that enthused about Merv's show, but it was better than nothing. We didn't have another TV to watch. Besides, Merv occasionally interviewed a cool guest, like Steve Majors, the "Six Million Dollar Man," or Henry Winkler, the "Fonz."

By the time Merv's show started each night, Dad had finished a quart or two of beer, his usual dosage. Dad was the most prone to losing his cool when the day and the bottles were nearly empty. So it was best to blend into the living room scenery when Merv took center stage.

One of Merv's guests got me into a heap of trouble: the Maharishi Mahesh Yogi, the founder of Transcendental Meditation, or TM. During one of Merv's shows, the Maharishi sat on what seemed to me a makeshift throne. He wore a white gown and a fresh flower lei. His long gray locks hung past his shoulders. He looked wise yet silly at the same time, sort of like Jimmy Carter. And from the royal way the Maharishi was presented and treated, you would have thought the guy were some sort of saint. But that couldn't be, for whatever the Maharishi was, it wasn't Catholic, that much I knew for sure. No collar. No crucifix. No pointy hat like the Pope's.

Spurred on in part by the Maharishi's Merv appearance, Dad took an interest in TM. Soon after, he signed up for and completed a six-week class and began meditating twice a day.

The religious overtones attached to the Maharishi seemed inappropriate and at odds with what I was being taught about not worshiping false gods. Had not these people seen *The Ten Commandments*, starring Charlton Heston?

Dad's fascination with TM was another reminder that my parents didn't practice their faith—*my* faith—anymore. This created some separation between them and me. I was seeking to get closer to the very thing they seemed to be moving away from. I envied those kids whose families worshiped together. Surrounded by such families in church, I felt a bit embarrassed there sans parents. Mine were, at best, lazy, at worst, pagans. In either case, their nonpracticing status wasn't helping me any.

Convinced that he was smarter, more energetic, and just an all-around better person as a meditator, Dad enrolled his wife and kids in the next round of TM classes. Becoming one with the universe was going to be a family project.

The TM course was held inside an ornate, empty mansion in Walnut Hills, a well-to-do part of town that I wasn't familiar with. The home smelled liked lemons from all the polish used to keep the wood floors and trim as shiny as the chrome on my bike. The instructor, Lester Warman, was a handsome, well-dressed man in his thirties who radiated the confidence and inner peace TM was said to deliver. He lived in Spain, but was in the states teaching for the Maharishi. On each tan hand he wore several gold rings. They flashed in the light as Lester tried to convey a sense of TM's "buzz" by twirling each hand, one clockwise, the other counterclockwise, next to his head.

"TM will relax your mind so deeply it will release your full potential," Lester said to the group of twenty, most nodding in anticipation. My head did not move. "You'll be able to live life on a different plane and get in touch with your essential nature," he continued. Some losers even took notes. "Expect to find yourself."

Find yourself? Jesus, I thought, how bad off did one have to be if he had to find himself? Was it possible to be that lost? I couldn't imagine it.

Lester's cobalt-blue eyes, square chin, and confident demeanor lent a forcefulness to everything he said. I bet that he could talk anyone into anything. I was on to him, though, my guard up. As Lester talked, his soothing voice and promises of ultimate contentment began to sound familiar, too familiar. Warning lights flashed in my head. This sort of talk about peace and happiness, when not spoken in church, was a clear sign. TM was a cult, I thought. And if it got out of hand, as cults have a tendency of doing, I could see my family traveling the country in the Beige Bomber recruiting for the Maharishi. I pictured myself in a robe standing outside a Steak 'n' Shake in Des Moines passing out flowers and fliers.

"Would you like to experience inner peace?" I'd ask some man with a friendly face as he walked out eager to get dinner home to his family.

"I beg your pardon?" he'd say.

"Would you like to get in touch with your true self?"

"Step aside, I'm in a hurry, kid."

I'd follow my prospect to his car, continuing my sales pitch. "I'm talking about TM, man, Transcendental Meditation," I'd say to his back. "It will blow your mind. *At least* take a flier."

"No thanks, I'll stick to my religion," he'd say, while stepping into his car.

"Who needs religion when you can find the god inside you? It worked for the Beatles, man! You know, John, Paul, George, and Ringo!"

My recruit, now inside his car, would roll down his window, begrudgingly take my flier and then ask, "Where are your parents?"

"That's them over there next to that VW. Hey, do you need a pair of Earth Shoes? It's the natural way to walk, you know." My prospect would drive away, his head shaking. In a desperate last attempt to make contact, I'd yell in vain, "I noticed your posture could use some help!"

To make myself feel better about my family's nomadic life, I'd remind myself that at least I was seeing the country. I'd then spot another potential convert carrying a sack of beef and give my speech another shot.

Daydreaming of this sort helped me tune out most of what Lester was laying on us. At least God knew that I was mocking this TM hogwash. The Devil also helped keep my mind off inner peace. Not the least bit to my surprise, he paid a visit during one of the TM classes. During this visit, as with some of the others to follow, I could smell gasoline. It was more like tasting it in the back of my mouth. I would have swore—probably taking the Lord's name in vain—that someone was pumping gas right there in the room.

Satan flew away as quickly as he came, leaving me with a headache and, for the first time, with thoughts that perhaps I should just come clean about my demonic possession before Dad unwittingly led me not to the peace and quiet of meditation, but to the crying and screaming of the eternally damned. Surely the Maharishi, a funny-looking, funny-talking man in robe, sandals, and flower leis was up to no good. But I kept my mouth shut. I may have been sliding down a slippery slope to Hades, but I wasn't quite up for a confrontation with Dad about his meditating. I could tell he was really fired up about this TM stuff. Any attempt to tell him that he was wrong was sure to lead to serious protest and, after he had a beer or two, an even more serious lecture about being open to new things and, more importantly, doing what your parents ask you. I would rather receive wedgies in gym class than suffer through those "talks."

And if I were to tell Mom that Satan were controlling me like a marionette, she would just laugh and tell me not to worry about it, that I was just letting my imagination get away from me. Again.

By this point I was silently praying every night in bed. Praying aloud would not have been a cool thing; Catholics leave that for church. Besides, I couldn't seem too interested in prayer; it would raise suspicions. So I prayed under my blankets, careful not to blow my cover under the covers.

After six evening TM classes, Mom, my siblings, and I were deemed ready to "graduate," obtain our secret mantras, and join Dad—and Merv—in the pursuit of better karma. A special ceremony was to be held at the mansion the following Saturday. We were instructed to bring fruit and flowers with us for the "service." This only heightened my anxiety over worshiping someone and something I knew I shouldn't. It didn't kill the Beatles, so I thought maybe I'd be OK. But I wasn't sure.

I was happy to be done with the course, but worried what demons might be called forth when I was invited into a room with Lester to receive my mantra, that meaningless word meditators focus on in order to clear their minds. Going one-on-one with Lester brought back memories of stepping into the confessional box at church for the first time, my knees weak, the urge to puke quite strong.

On TM graduation day, each student brought some fruit and flower offerings. It reminded me of school Masses during which select students bring the "gifts" of bread, wine, and water to the altar. For my mantra ceremony, I brought an apple, an orange, and a tulip—and a prayer that I would not be struck dead. I noticed when I walked into the mansion that a couple of garden gargoyles looked like mad cows. Moses had to contend with golden calves; mine were concrete.

As my family stepped into the mansion, a nerdy-looking woman with crooked teeth and a flower crown instructed us to be quiet. Something very special, sacred even, was happening here, we were told. And something very evil, I thought.

We sat still as cats in one of the side rooms and waited our turns with Lester. I wondered if he had seen the disbelief in my eyes during his lectures, and if so, what he might say to me when he had me all alone. My stomach queasy, I imagined the words Lester and I might exchange:

"At last we're alone," he'd say, his tan hands clasped together, his eyes, as bright blue as those fake rocks found in the bottom of aquariums, piercing me. "I've been wanting to ask you some questions."

"Like what?" I'd ask, looking away.

"Like why have you been so uneasy in class?"

"Mom says I'm naturally nervous," I'd say, shrugging my shoulders and lifting my hands.

"So you're open to freeing your mind?"

"Uh, I suppose."

"You're prepared to recognize the genius of the Maharishi?" Lester would ask in my daydream, nodding toward a photo of the Bearded One.

"I dig his robe."

"You didn't answer the question."

"I'm Catholic. I can only worship God, Jesus, or the Holy Spirit. Of course I can pray to Mary and the saints, too."

"I'm not concerned with the other world, assuming it even exists," Lester would say, shrugging. "I just want you to be happy in this one."

"Oh, I am. Can I have my mantra now?"

Just then in my dream, Sister Lucy busts in and whacks Lester over the head with a gallon bottle of holy water, a rosary wound tightly in her other hand. And I run out of the house, Sister Lucy clearing a path ahead of me, my family in hot pursuit, the Beige Bomber waiting out front, its little engine running and ready for a speedy getaway. I'd then be in the cubbyhole, flipping Lester off out the back window.

My little fantasy came to an abrupt end when Dad, all smiles, asked me if I was ready for my mantra. I told him yes, because I couldn't tell him anything else. Mom entered the mantra room first. Five minutes later, she came out looking, as usual, as if she might start laughing. Larry, a sarcastic kid with freckles, dark red hair, and really white teeth, then walked in and came out with a blank look on his face that was born of either boredom or fear. And I wasn't able to talk to either Mom or Larry. They had to begin meditating immediately while their new mantras were fresh. Poor Dave and Teri had to wait even longer than I did.

Lester's helper, a pretty college student in a long, flowery gown and sandals, summoned me. I shuffled into the room, hoping that Lester's aide wouldn't leave. But she did. Hanging before me was a large framed photograph of the Maharishi, draped in purple cloth the same shade as the priests' vestments at St. William. A dozen candles and overpowering incense reminded me of Catholic funerals and holy day Masses.

I expected lightning to strike.

Lester, decked out in a red robe and black sandals and sitting cross-legged on a large pillow, asked me to sit beside him. He took my apple, orange, and tulip and placed them at the makeshift altar. He then began to jabber in a foreign language. I thought I heard something like it in school during a National Geographic film. Lester bowed a few times and lit another candle. He then asked if I was ready for my mantra. I nodded, too afraid to speak.

Lester asked me to repeat my mantra aloud with him several times. He then shook my hand, welcomed me to the world of TM, and then invited me to go meditate and experience life on a different plane, whatever that meant. I found a seat along a bay window and closed my eyes. My heart began to settle and I found it a bit easier to breathe.

I decided to give meditation a whirl for fear Lester or Dad would be able to tell that I hadn't tried. But my mantra, "ing," got in the way. It didn't help relax my mind but rather aroused it—and other parts—for "ing" was just one syllable away from

57

squeez*ing*, lick*ing*, kiss*ing*, and other choice verbs of this horny twelve-year-old.

In the following weeks, about the only thing TM heightened was my newfound sex drive. By this point I considered TM more amusing than anything, and realized that the Pope had nothing to worry about when it came to Merv or the Maharishi.

At Dad's insistence, my brother Larry and I meditated after school before going out to play. Dave and Teri, too young to be expected to sit still for very long, were given "walking mantras." They could meditate while strolling to a friend's house to play Battleship or to the store to buy some Tootsie-Rolls. Larry and I were beside ourselves with envy.

Our initial meditation sessions lasted about twenty minutes. Before long, Larry and I were pleading for shorter sentences, especially on nice days. Neither of us found meditating peaceful, just frustrating. We could hear the squeals of delight coming from other kids playing outside. I spent the time thinking about homework, rockets, and most of all, girls, my growing reason for be–*ing*.

Mom didn't seem to enjoy TM either. She lost interest even faster than Larry and me. Within a couple of weeks, the daily meditation became an every-other-day affair. And then a weekly affair. And then a past affair. We all stopped meditating, Dad the longest holdout, of course. He kept at it for about six months before getting bored and seeking higher levels of mental clarity through more running and juicing. At least his bowels would be clear, I thought.

Things were looking up. I looked a false god in the eyes and survived to tell the tale. This whole TM thing also helped me realize that Satan could influence events from many different vantage points, television included.

It was a dangerous world no matter how you looked at it.

Chapter 8

Triple the Fun

My life had turned into one big score sheet, a running tally between the forces of good and evil. I'd help my mom with the dishes and earn a good point. I'd fight with my sister and earn a bad point. I'd say a prayer and add a good point. I'd think of Gail, get all tingly inside, and add a bad point—sometimes two or three.

One of the easiest and quickest means I had to secure protection against Satan was crossing myself. It only took two seconds to say, "In the name of the Father, the Son, and the Holy Spirit," while touching my forehead, stomach, left and then right shoulder. But since excessive crossing could arouse suspicion, I crossed myself in silence and without the hand gestures. Unless, of course, I was alone or in church. And I seldom crossed just once, but rather three times, nine times, fifteen times. Whatever it took. But always—always—a multiple of three, God's number, and never six, the Devil's digit.

While watching an episode of *Columbo* on TV and hearing the phrase "double-crossed," I realized that I could increase the protective powers of crossing by doing it twice, once forward and then once backward. Although I crossed—and double-crossed—myself at least three times a day, I had no idea what the Trinity really meant. I did, however, think the Pope or whoever thought it up was brilliant.

The Trinity gave me three gods for the price of one. Who could argue with that? If I upset the Son, I could appeal to the Father or even the Holy Spirit. Just like when I was on the outs with Dad, I could approach Mom with my request for candy money or bus fare for a trip downtown. When my pleas fell short with Mom *and* Dad, Grandma Marge was always good for a couple of coins. Given my mounting moral weaknesses, I needed such options among my heavenly and earthly guardians.

Nonstop crossing and double-crossing served as a constant reminder that the number three held special power and meaning. After all, God was three people in one. I never quite grasped this mystery, but I thought of it as Neapolitan ice cream. The Father was the chocolate, the dominant color; the Son was the strawberry, the closest to blood red; and the Holy Spirit was vanilla, the color of doves.

Much of what was important seemed to come in threes. Jesus was dead for three days before rising. My parents had three sons. Malts came in three sizes: small, medium, and large. There were three kinds of girls: ugly ones, "dogs"; nice ones, "goodie-two-shoes"; and bad ones, "sluts." Grandma Marge always said certain things happen in threes: celebrity deaths, natural disasters, and Grandpa's bouts with irritable bowel syndrome.

As I understood it, there were three major world religions: Catholics, Protestants, and Jews. These three faiths covered the gamut of religious options. You could either believe in the Trinity and the Pope as the Catholics did, just believe in the Trinity as the Protestants did, or just God as the Jews did.

My crossing and double-crossing seemed to increase in direct relation to my feelings for girls. The sixth grade is when I remember discovering just how wonderful girls could actually be. This was a major paradigm shift, kind of like when you realize that some vegetables actually taste pretty good. Just a year before, I was more interested in doing and saying things that would make girls describe me as "super gross" or "very immature." Either badge of honor would do. And my friends and I weren't afraid to use water balloons, dead spiders, or wads of green phlegm culled from the bottom of our lungs to offend and irritate.

But then, in sixth grade, I was not only interested in getting girls' attention, but their affection, too. The first object of my desire was Gail Gruber. Her short hair was as black as the cinders on a running track, her eyes hazel, and her skin a light brown. Her best attribute, however, was her deadly spitball aim and her willingness to act up in class and irritate the teacher. Gail was the ideal first crush. She looked like a girl, but she acted like a boy. This was undoubtedly the best combination since some genius at the Charms candy company combined the lollipop with bubble gum to create the Blow Pop.

Gail and I would occasionally pass notes in class, but she preferred to talk on the phone. Thing was, in my family's small apartment, the phone sat in the dining room, positioned between the kitchen and the living room. Anything you said on the phone was public property as far as Mom was concerned. Using that sixth sense that only mothers seemed to have, she noticed immediately if I was on the phone with a girl. And when she did, Mom dropped whatever she was doing and took an immediate interest in dusting. With her back toward me, she hovered close enough to pick up interesting tidbits, which she then teased me about mercilessly.

"Stevie's got a girlfriend, and they're going to meet on the playground tomorrow, and maybe kissy, kissy," she said, over and over and *over*. At first I'd ignore her taunts, and then, agitated, deny them. When she kept up, I'd get so furious that I'd stomp off admitting she was right, except for the kissy, kissy part, of course. To keep this kind of harassment to a minimum, I took to calling Gail from one of the neighborhood phone booths.

"Hi Gail, it's Steve," I said, straining to deepen my voice without sounding like it.

"Where are you?" she asked, her voice sweeter and warmer than hot chocolate with marshmallows.

"Home."

"It's really loud."

"Our windows are open."

"In this weather? It must be freezing."

"Mom just washed the carpets and wanted to dry them," I said, trying to keep my teeth from chattering. The cold, hard plastic phone against my ear sent chills down my spine. "So how'd you do on the m-m-math quiz?" I said, trying to change the subject.

I increased my daily quotas for signing and praying to make up for the impure thoughts that my newfound interest in the opposite sex inspired (as well as the extra coins I was stealing from Mom to feed the pay phone).

My life had turned into one big score sheet, a running tally between the forces of good and evil. I'd help my mom with the dishes and earn a good point. I'd fight with my sister and earn a bad point. I'd say a prayer and add a good point. I'd think of Gail, get all tingly inside, and add a bad point—sometimes two or three. It was hard keeping tabs on an exact score, but it was clear that I had more bad points than good, for the Devil kept coming, even at church, the worst possible sign.

One Friday morning I stood in the sacristy in my black cassock and white surplice, my hands folded at my waist. My serving partner didn't show up, a common occurrence at the six-thirty morning Mass. I watched Father Lisper, a tiny, soft-spoken man we altar boys called "Father Whisper," put on his vestments. I turned my head to catch a glimpse of the morning sun coming through one of the sacristy's intricate stained-glass windows. Just then, Satan arrived. And I left the real world and traveled through hell, everything mean and nasty, not because I saw angry monsters, but because my mind was being violated, forced to see stuff, strange stuff, stuff that I didn't need to see, that I didn't *want* to see. Especially in church.

After this visit, as with most, I felt off my game for a few hours, my mind in need of some oil, some bolt tightening, and a good polishing just as my bike often did. The feeling, or mood, was like that strange déjà vu sensation, but one with more punch. The visit also inspired a headache, which would happen now and then after visits. My head would usually begin hurting about a half-hour later, right when my new habit—rapidly rubbing my palms together—was in full motion.

"Are you okay?" Father Whisper asked right at the end of the episode.

"Huh?" I responded, clearly startled.

"Are you okay, son?"

"Yes, Father. I was . . . I was . . . praying, just praying."

"Looked more like sleeping to me," Father said with a barely audible chuckle.

"No, just praying."

"Which prayer?"

"The Prayer of St. Francis, Father."

"'Lord, make me an instrument of your peace'," he said, quoting the first part. "It's one of my favorites. You sure you're okay?"

"Yes, Father," I said, turning away from him for fear my eyes would tell the truth. I thought about telling him. No doubt all the tools were nearby for an exorcism: incense, holy water, as well as crucifixes for me to barf on. But I dismissed the idea, as there was too much to lose. My excuse would cover me, thank God. Though distracted after Satan's visits, I could still tell stories. In fact, telling stories, or getting back to whatever it is I was doing, helped me to feel like my old self again.

"Well then," Father said, "let's get started."

We walked to the edge of the altar where I pulled on a red ornamental rope attached to a golden bell about the size of a basketball. The ring signaled to the two dozen people in the pews that they should stand, since the Mass was beginning. The heavy clang just inches from my aching head felt like someone had taken a skillet to the back of my skull.

Father Whisper and I walked slowly to the front of the altar. My hands, flat together and pointing heavenward, shook a little. We bowed before the altar. Bending over made my head feel like it was going to plop off. Father Whisper took his position front and center; I walked to the side of the altar where the servers positioned themselves. There, I offered my suffering up to heaven, in the name of the Father, Son, and Holy Spirit. I then asked that one of the Three show his gratitude and stop the Devil's visits.

Chapter 9

The Thrill of Victory

I decided then to embark on a training program befitting an Olympic athlete. A stronger body would not only please the Lord but also make it more difficult for the Devil to penetrate my flesh. Hardened muscles and ultra-efficient lungs would be my shield.

As promised, Tom Norton, the high school student who had coached our track team to embarrassment the previous year, returned. This time we had not one, but two weeks to prepare for the championship meet. Practically enough to get ready for the Olympics. The more serious approach to our training included walking to Rapid Run Park and jogging the cross-country course used by Elder High School's team. Dubbed the "Purple Pack" after the school's color and tight-knit culture, Elder's cross-country team was a state powerhouse, Coach Norton told us.

The freshly cut grass at Rapid Run smelled especially vibrant. And the spring-soaked turf under my yellow gym shoes made me feel heavier, stronger. As we intermittently jogged and walked the course, I noticed that I could keep up with everyone on the team, even the eighth graders. Some of them asked for breaks. I still felt fresh. I dreamed then of joining the Purple Pack when I entered Elder. I would run over hill and dale in the name of Jesus, my uniform a shiny purple, the color that I most associated with the King of Kings.

But first things first, I thought. I and the rest of the team had to stay focused on the Catholic schools championship meet. We knew that training was important to our success. Though the spirit was willing, the flesh was weak. When left unsupervised at Rapid Run one practice, we opted to spend our time on the playground equipment rather than the cross-country course. "Pumping your legs hard while you swing is a great workout, too," one of our teammates said in a matter-of-fact tone. It made sense to all of us. We did, however, manage to get in a bit of running during the supervised practice sessions.

On the big day, our team still didn't sport uniforms, but at least no one wore dress shoes. And since we expected the affluent parishes to show up in their color-coordinated shirts and jerseys, we were neither surprised nor psyched out. We walked around Roger Bacon High School's stadium with our chests out, our physiques well-shaped, we thought, by a bit of running and some power playground swinging. Our confidence, however flimsily rooted in reality, paid off. We St. William's Barons scored points in several events. Though I really only cared about one: the two-mile relay. I and the other three relay team members would each run two laps, a half-mile.

Once again, I ran the third leg. Perfect, I thought. God would opt for the third leg if he were running. "It's the most important leg, the one where races are won and lost," Coach Norton told me, his arm around my shoulder, when no one else was within earshot. (I took great pride in this before the race, though I learned afterward that the coach told everyone on my relay team the same thing about *his* leg of the relay.)

I walked around the infield and said three extra "Hail Marys" and three "Our Fathers" before the gun went off. Even before my teammate completed the first lap, I could see that this race was going to be different than last year's. We were going to be contenders, which meant *I* was going to be a contender.

While the first and second runners completed their laps, I paced. I squeezed in three more "Hail Marys" right before the baton was handed to me. We were in ninth place. We needed to finish in seventh or better to score points—and get a ribbon. I took the first half of the first lap a bit too quickly, but then found my rhythm. "Pace yourself!" "Keep it up!" "Get the lead out!" I heard as I passed the start/finish line in front of the stands after my first lap. Mom and Dad cheered me on, too. I tried to aim a smile in their direction.

In the back stretch of the second lap, my knees locked up and my lungs felt as if they had turned to lead. My mouth was dry and my tongue felt twice its normal size. I could hear some shouts coming from the stands across the football field, but I couldn't make out anything specific. I felt detached from the world, too tired to do anything but command my legs to put one in front of the other, and pray they obeyed.

My competitors were older and bigger and some were way out ahead. But others were actually *behind* me. I did manage to keep us in ribbon contention, passing the baton on to eighth grader Pat Callahan, our final and best runner, in ninth place. He was the poor sap who had to endure the embarrassment of having the stadium lights turned off on him at last year's meet. He was especially ready to run. And did he ever.

I fell to the infield to catch my breath, my legs incapable of doing anything, even standing. The fifteen other members of St.

William's team were cheering Pat on, oblivious to my pain. I felt happy, though, too. We were beating some of the paneled-basement parishes despite their fast, flashy uniforms.

Pat finished in sixth place, scoring the four of us a purple ribbon. For the first time, I tasted victory in athletic competition. Now I understood what all my previous coaches and teammates got so excited about. I would never hear the weekly introduction to *Wide World of Sports* the same way again. I had heretofore known only the agony of defeat. Now I knew the thrill of victory, or at least one of her cousins.

On the way home after the meet, I sat in back of the Beige Bomber. I felt tired yet perfectly content. I caressed my purple ribbon, the silky texture nearly erotic. Dad talked on and on about the meet and my fine performance. He and Mom were taking me to Graeters, the ice cream shop of special occasions.

Jesus was certainly pleased, too. But he would be even more so if I were to be victorious someday in a purer, truer sense: first place and the coveted blue ribbon. I wanted a chance to really train and then run against kids my own age. Encouraged by my team's achievement, I believed that a first-place ribbon could someday be within my reach. I decided then to embark on a training program befitting an Olympic athlete. A stronger body would not only please the Lord but also make it more difficult for the Devil to penetrate my flesh. Hardened muscles and ultra-efficient lungs would be my shield.

From the first few miles, I knew that my running was not only a means of staying healthy, strong, and nimble, it was also another calculated move to gain Dad's approval, to stay on his good side, to keep things calm. I recalled the Bible mentioning that Jesus said, "Blessed are the peacemakers." I would learn years later that the children of alcoholics often become such hungry pleasers that they'll do about anything to avoid rocking the boat or creating a confrontation. We're used to tip-toeing around, holding our breath, and lying low. Dad couldn't have been more delighted with my newfound interest in running. What father doesn't want to share his passion with his children? To Dad's credit, though, he never pushed me the way you hear about some overzealous parents doing, eager to create the next music or sports whiz.

But my primary motivation for running was to strengthen my body in order to discourage Satan *and* to taste again the sweet nectar of victory, or at least near victory.

Every day after school, I put on my running clothes, did my homework, and then watched cartoons or painted one of my model rockets while I waited for Dad. The bus dropped him off at about four-thirty in front of our house. He'd change his clothes and then we would walk down our front stairs and out the door. We began running the moment our feet hit the concrete walk at the base of our front porch's wooden steps. (Stretching first wasn't part of Dad's routine, so it wasn't part of mine.)

Dad had a favorite five-mile course, which ran through Rapid Run Park and the campus of what had been the Dunham Tuberculosis Hospital. I tried not to breathe in too deeply when we ran by the vacated buildings. I couldn't risk inhaling some left-over germs that might weaken my lungs and, thereby, reduce my chances at running glory.

When I first began running with Dad, I would turn around after about a mile. I'd jog and walk home while Dad completed his course. After a couple of months of slowly increasing my endurance and confidence, I developed to the point where I could run the entire five miles with Dad every day.

As we ran, we listened to music on Dad's transistor radio that he carried in his right hand. Songs such as Elton John's "Philadelphia Freedom," Glen Campbell's "Rhinestone Cowboy," and, ironically, Van McCoy's "The Hustle" provided a beat for our feet. We talked, mostly about track and field and our running heroes, people such as Jim Ryun, Steve Prefontaine, and Mary Decker. Our banter, like our legs, slowing as we trudged uphill.

"You seem to be handling the hills better," Dad said, after we crested one by the old hospital.

"I'm leaning into them." Deep breath. "Just like you told me to."

"That's good," Dad said, taking a deep breath of his own. "But don't clench your fists."

"It helps me pump my arms harder," I said, exaggerating my arm movements.

"Stay loose, you'll conserve energy."

"Sure." Deep breath. "Loose as a goose."

During the end of one of our jaunts, Dad said, "There's a fun-run this weekend at Sharon Woods. Wanna go?"

Fun-runs weren't officially races, but rather an opportunity to run with others over a measured course and get timed. I wasn't ready for a real race yet, but I was intrigued by the fun-run concept.

"How long is it?" I asked.

"You can pick. A half-mile or five miles."

"I'll do the half-mile I guess."

"Maybe you should try *both*."

"Maybe," I said. "What times should I shoot for?"

"Three minutes for the half-mile and about thirty-five minutes for the five-mile," Dad said. "Think you can do it?"

"Is the course hilly or flat?"

"Mostly flat."

"Then probably."

"It's all about pacing yourself."

"I will."

"I'll race you to that light," Dad said pointing toward a pole fifty yards ahead. Dad would often challenge me to a sprint. He had considerable leg speed, something I wouldn't be able to match for years, and even then it was a photo finish. And, to this day, I'm not absolutely sure that he didn't let me win. In fact, I would bet that he did. This is the kind of fatherly love that always managed to, in the big picture, overshadow his alcohol-induced outbursts, like the time he ripped into me for talking too loud on the phone when he was trying to nap. He was probably hungover, oddly enough, a rarity.

I did participate in the fun-run that weekend. I missed my three-minute target for the half-mile run by just thee seconds. However, I beat my thirty-five-minute target for the five-mile run by nearly a minute and a half. Dad and I celebrated with breakfast at the Waffle House. Heavy butter. Heavy syrup.

The training with Dad continued. During one of our runs, he brought along his hand-held, silent Super-8 movie camera. We took turns filming each other running up and down hills in Rapid Run Park. After a few minutes of serious footage, we then—at

One of the first tangible signs of my running abilities.

Dad's direction and instigation—began to run in zigzag patterns like we had just stepped off a carnival Tilt-o-Whirl. We fell to the ground and tossed our legs up in the air. We also pretended to run into trees and fall backward on our butts, shaking our heads as if seeing stars. I felt like a cartoon character.

At other sports, and even life in general, I didn't have to pretend to mess things up. It happened naturally. Like when I visited a riverside park with a friend and fell into the Ohio River. Fortunately the friend's older brother was with us. He was an Eagle Scout and a lifeguard. He knew just what to do to keep me from floating downstream.

But running, well, that was different. It came easy.

Filming Dad acting crazy in a good way served to bring into deeper relief his acting crazy in the bad way. Dad was a complex guy. A meditator and a screamer. A health-food nut and a drinker. Almost always a caring, happy man but sometimes a mean, bitter one. It made no sense from one perspective, but all the sense in the world from another. Everything had both a good and a bad side. With girls in skirts and math tests, school certainly did. With my eagerness to serve Jesus *and* my demonic possession, I most certainly did, too.

As I think back upon my regular workouts with Dad, I count my blessings for all our runs, blessings that total more than the thousands of miles we logged together. This running of ours was true quality time. We were more than father and son. We were two guys running toward something. Dad toward better health, me toward blue ribbons and white-hot purity. Of course, I now see that we were both running away from something, too. Dad from whatever it was that made him drink and act like a jerk, me from impending doom.

It didn't take long for my classmates and others in the neighborhood to see me running around the neighborhood with Dad.

Most seemed to admire my endurance, even if they couldn't understand the allure of distance running. I would rather have been a star player in one of the premier sports, that is, one with a ball. But I had to play the hand that was dealt me. It could have been worse, I thought. I could have discovered that I had an aptitude for figure skating.

Once, when running alone because Dad had another commitment, I noticed my former baseball coach cutting his grass. I could tell from about fifty yards away that I caught his attention, too. He stopped mowing and just stared, probably not believing that this most uncoordinated of kids was actually out running, moving steadily, effortlessly—and forward, too. I picked up the pace a little. I ran right by him, neither of us acknowledging the other. The road dipped down then back up in such a way that he could see me another four hundred yards later. I glanced back. He was still watching. None of his players, even the very good ones, could do what I was now doing. And I didn't need a ball, a bat—or even a coach—to do it.

I liked to be seen out running. It was something no other kid in my school was doing at the time. I was different. Special. I thanked God for inventing running and bringing it to me. I was prepared to run my legs off for his glory—and some of my own.

If I were going to be Satan's target, I'd at least be a moving one.

Chapter 10

Media Attention

> When you're hiding a big secret, the last person you want to hear from is a member of the media. Jim missed the big story that day, I thought to myself in bed that night. I imagined the interview as it could have gone if Jim knew what my running was really about.

Many of Dad's colorful friends were fellow patrons at his favorite watering hole: Dase's Place. The owner, Denny Dase, weighed three hundred pounds. An outstanding prep football player in the early sixties, Denny was recruited by Arizona State. However, his gridiron career came to an unfortunate end during his sophomore year when a brain aneurysm required an extensive operation. Denny was left prone to seizures and watching football from the stands.

Denny was baldheaded with a goatee, the scars from his brain surgery clearly visible. He stood like a rounder, shorter Frankenstein without the green skin, while trophies and team photos from his extinct football career gathered dust behind him on the liquor rack. His scars eerily reflected the light from neon signs overhead, making him seem all the more menacing and oddly mysterious. I bet he could squash Volkswagens with his bare hands. And then eat the scrap metal if he wanted.

I wished that some sort of surgery could eliminate my demons. But I knew better. Doctors could remove my brain entirely. It wouldn't matter. Satan was in my soul. No doctor was going to touch the Evil Ghost with a scalpel. If only it were that easy. I wouldn't have minded the scars. They would have made me look tough, just like Denny.

Dad occasionally brought me to Dase's Place on Saturday afternoons. The bar was long and skinny and always smoky, cool, and dark, even on the brightest afternoons. My first stop was usually the jukebox. I wasn't interested in the fifties and sixties tunes available for play, but I dipped my finger into the change return and always found at least a dollar in coins abandoned by the patrons too distracted or drunk to know better. As Dad and I hung out listening to stories of athletic conquest, he drank beer, I Cokes, which always tasted better when sipping them perched upon a barstool, a swizzle stick poking out the top of my glass. Dad's drinking never seemed anything but fun at Dase's. I looked forward to the day when I could spend all my free time in a bar, drinking the adult drinks, yucking it up with the bartender and my stool mates.

Dase's Place attracted its fair share of real athletes, wannabe athletes, and washed-up athletes. Dougie Seibert, one of the regulars at Dase's Place, was once a hockey champion in Canada who, in a drunken stupor as a young man, fell off of a bridge and broke his back. The serious spine and head injuries put Dougie's hockey career on ice. Dad brought Dougie home for a meal now and then, usually a frozen pizza Mom warmed in the oven. My siblings and I would sit around the table, pretending not to stare at Dougie as he raised a slice of pizza to his mouth, his hand shaking, drool dripping from his lower lip.

Dougie liked to show off a tattered black-and-white photo of himself on the ice, his stick between his hands the way a cocky cop holds a billy club. The photo of Dougie's once fast and energetic physique contrasted so sharply with his slow speech and worn-out body that it nearly brought me to tears. Dougie would talk about his glory days. I was never quite sure how much of his slurred speech to attribute to his physical ailments and how much to chalk up to too much beer. He was just so damn pathetic. I remember feeling warm about Dad for the kindness he showed Dougie. It seemed like something Jesus would do.

The sport of choice at Dase's was arm wrestling. The tiny joint would pack them in on weekends for local and regional meets. These attracted crowds similar in looks and smells to those I would have expected to find at a biker rally. It wasn't unusual for some to check guns at the door.

Denny was a fierce competitor, in the heavyweight division, of course. Dad told me that Denny once broke some guy's arm in a competition. "Cool," I said. "I wish I'd seen that."

In addition to arm wrestling, the regulars at Dase's Place served up all kinds of offbeat feats and challenges for other patrons. I witnessed Denny attempt the world record for speed-eating ice cream. He missed by less than a pint. But he redeemed himself just minutes later by breaking the record for speed-eating pickled onions. His accomplishment was recorded on film and verified via the notarized signatures of Dad and a handful of drunks. I would rather have seen record-breaking sword swallowing or Evel Knievel jump buses, but it was cool to witness Denny inhale food and later read his name in that bible of exceptional human talent: *The Guinness Book of World Records*.

Though Dad didn't arm wrestle, he was well-liked at Dase's Place. Not to be left out of the fun and games, Dad invited others to join him for a run up Straight Street, a half-mile long road so named because it rises nearly vertical. To make the challenge even more entertaining bar banter, Dad decided that the run up Straight Street would happen *backward*. After that steep climb, and without rest, Dad and anyone brave enough to join him would, facing forward, then jog a mile to the University of Cincinnati's thirty-thousand-seat football stadium, where they would run up and down all the stairs. Then Dad and his guests would, also without resting, conclude the challenge with a forward five-mile run around the bar's hilly neighborhood. Illustrated handbills encouraging people to join Dad were posted in the bar.

No one accepted Dad's challenge. But he did it anyway. No problem.

Dad would often boast about my latest running achievements to Denny and the others warming the barstools. "Steve ran five miles in under thirty-five minutes," Dad said once. Denny winked and congratulated me in his deep, calm voice. He'd pour me another Coke, wipe down the bar with a rag, and then toss me a bag of M&M's.

Though proud of my achievements, I was sometimes embarrassed by the way Dad gushed over me. I both liked and hated the attention. At the end of the day, there were only four, maybe five, people who needed to know about my running: Jesus, Satan, and my parents. The possible fifth was whatever girl was the object of my affections that month. Talking me up to Denny and some Saturday afternoon drunks was one thing, but bragging about me in front of the whole world was something else altogether. And it happened early in my seventh grade year, just days before the Labor Day break and an important race.

I was sitting at the kitchen table, eating my bowl of Wheaties when the phone rang, always unusual and worrisome at 7:30 A.M. Mom picked the phone up in the living room, said, "Hello," and then, "Why, yes, he'd *love* to talk to you." She held her hand over the phone and yelled for me in the kitchen. I walked toward her, a bad feeling in my gut. "It's for you, Stevie," she said, a suspicious smile on her face, shoving the phone toward me. I expected to hear a girl's voice on the other end and then watch Mom mouth silently "I love you" and blow kisses into the air.

"Hello," I said, tentatively, turning my back toward Mom.

"Is this Steve Kissing, the long-distance runner?" It was a man's voice, a smooth one, at once familiar and out of place. It was too old to be a friend. And it didn't sound like any priest, teacher, or other adult I knew.

"Yes, this is him, I mean me," I said, turning around to look at Mom to get a clue of some sort. She just stood there, grinning, shrugging her shoulders.

"This is Jim Scott at WSAI. I understand you have a big race this weekend."

Oh my God! Dad gushed about me to the most popular morning DJ in town. *Everybody* listened to Jim Scott. How embarrassing!

"Yeah, the race is Saturday," I said, shooting an evil stare at Mom.

"Tell me about it."

"Uh, well, it's a four-mile cross-country race at French Park." What else was there to say? Who cares? Why did Dad do this?

"I hear it's a tough course?"

"Yeah, it's very hilly."

"You plan to win it?"

"I don't know. Maybe. I mean, I hope to do well in my age division."

"Your Dad says you run five miles a day. Is that your secret?"

If it was a secret, it wasn't any more. "I guess. And we run a lot of hills."

"You eat Wheaties every morning?"

I laughed a little because I was actually eating Wheaties, not that any one listening to the radio could see that.

"Well, keep up with your training. I understand that you'll soon be running for the famed 'Purple Pack.'"

I turned my back toward Mom. "I hope so. In a couple of years." Running for Elder High School was my dream. To hear it spoken of so matter-of-factly as if it were sure to happen took me a bit off-guard. I felt charged up, yet also vulnerable and exposed. If I didn't make the team, now the whole wide world would know.

"Well, I wish you the best of luck."

"Thanks."

I hung up the phone. Mom kept smiling and turned the radio up so we could all hear the recorded interview a few minutes later. Hall & Oates sang "Rich Girl."

"I can't believe Dad did that!" I said, plunking myself back down with a grunt in front of my Wheaties.

"What's the problem?" Mom asked. "Your Dad thought it would be a nice thing."

"I sounded stupid." My brothers and sister grinned, intrigued by the interview and pleased, as any sibling would be, to witness a brother publicly humiliated.

"You sounded just fine. You'll see," Mom said, putting away the cereal boxes.

"No I didn't. I *really* wish Dad didn't do that." I let out a big sigh. "Jeez."

"I don't care what you think, Stevie. I thought it was fun."

"Well, I wish he hadn't done it," I said, my head down. "He should have told me, at least."

"He wanted it to be a surprise."

Mom called Dad at work to let him know that Jim Scott had called and to be sure to listen carefully during the next few minutes.

I poked at my cereal, my appetite gone, waiting to hear the interview, hoping it wouldn't air. But it did. I thought I sounded funny, my voice didn't seem like mine. At least I didn't stutter or accidentally say a curse word, I thought. After the interview, Jim Scott added, live, "that's one impressive kid." I did like the sound of that. I hoped the Devil had his radio dial set to the same position.

I walked slowly to school, the other kids well ahead of me. I imagined everyone waiting for me outside, ready to ridicule me for sounding like an idiot. *"Yes, Mr. Scott, I am a runner and a moron."* But no. Not a word until the second class when two girls said they heard me on the radio and thought it was cool. A dozen more of my classmates made note of it throughout the day. They all thought the interview—and therefore *me*—quite neat. I felt better about it, though I still voiced disapproval when Dad came home from work. I couldn't let him off too easy.

When you're hiding a big secret, the last person you want to hear from is a member of the media. Jim missed the big story that day, I thought to myself in bed that night. I imagined the interview as it could have gone if Jim knew what my running was really about.

"Is this Steve Kissing?"

"Yes, yes it is."

"This is Jim Scott at WSAI. I understand you're possessed by the Devil."

"Well, yes, Jim, I am."

"You've been a naughty boy, haven't you?"

"Well, yes, Jim, I have."

"Tell us some of the bad things you have done."

"I've stolen snacks from other kids' lunch boxes, told dirty jokes in church, and imagined some girls naked."

"And what's this about dead gerbils?"

"Uh, no comment."

"You deserve to be punished, don't you?" Pause. "Don't *you*?"

"It's all my fault, all my fault."

Despite Dad embarrassing me, I managed to win my age division at the race, pulling away after cresting the steepest hill on the course, even though my spine felt like it was in my ankles.

My victory was a testament to my talent, a beacon to the world that I could do something well. And it was a warning to the Devil that I was willing to endure pain—and public humiliation. Good thing. I was going to have to do both.

Chapter 11

The Fires Within

> We were shown painfully clear pictures of penises and vaginas with sores of all sorts. Yet another reminder that if one doesn't do what God asks—stay celibate until marriage and then committed throughout—there would be hell to pay with a plague of warts on your privates. God meant business. No doubt about it.

Seventh grade at St. William included two rites of passage: the sacrament of confirmation, during which we renewed our baptismal commitment, and the infinitely more interesting day-long sex-ed program.

For the talk about the birds and the bees, the boys and girls were separated. We boys received the eye-opening instruction in the music room from a physician, an antiabortion activist, and Father Kennedy.

We were shown movies and filmstrips that described how a man and woman have intercourse, how an egg is fertilized, and how that egg grows into a baby ready to pop out for pictures about nine months later. The antiabortionist spoke about the deep, dark evil that is abortion. He told us of the horrible means doctors used to murder babies. And we were shown grotesque pictures of aborted fetuses. Even fallen-away Catholics knew that abortion was wrong. Mom had taken to wearing a bracelet in protest of the Supreme Court's decision to legalize abortion.

We boys were told that our feelings toward girls were normal. Yet we were also told that we shouldn't act on those feelings and have sex until we were married. First and foremost, premarital sex broke church teachings. Second, we risked impregnating the girl. And since abortion was never an option, such a predicament would mean giving a baby up for adoption. Or dropping out of school to care for it. Worst still, we risked contracting a sexually transmitted disease.

We were shown painfully clear pictures of penises and vaginas with sores of all sorts. Yet another reminder that if one doesn't do what God asks—stay celibate until marriage and then committed throughout—there would be hell to pay with a plague of warts on your privates. God meant business. No doubt about it.

We were told about the changes happening to our bodies: deeper voices, more hair, and the like. We were also told about changes happening to girls' bodies: hips, boobs, and menstruation. "Periods can make women mean as hell," Greg Teal said, sitting behind me. "When my mom's on hers, my dad says it's best not to be seen. Or heard. He just stays in the garage."

I had been introduced to the basic mechanics of sex three years earlier when Mom sat Larry and me down to explain the fundamentals. A couple years older, Larry was probably ready for the big talk. I, on the other hand, just found the whole deal amusing—and more than a tad bit disturbing. I thought that perhaps Mom was pulling another joke on me. I couldn't imagine a man and woman doing such a thing, especially *my* mom and *my* dad, *my* aunts and *my* uncles. And, as for *my* grandparents, forget about it!

I vowed then that I would never have intercourse.

Three years later in the sex-ed program, all bets were off. Kind of. I had little interest in having premarital sex, such a sin would prove too crushing—and the penis warts too painful. Premarital sex would be equivalent to just giving in, to resigning my soul to Satan, who would sometimes come a couple of times a week. So I decided that I would be satisfied with just kissing a girl, and maybe rubbing up against one. But even then I knew I had to be careful or I would arouse more of Satan's interest.

During the sex-ed program we boys passed around jokes and limericks. Lenny Wilderman, a class clown among class clowns, with a devilish grin to boot, kept my attention divided between an occasional bare breast on the film strip screen and his funny commentary, which amounted to rhyming dirty words and inventing nicknames for body parts.

In spite of the distractions, we made it through the rest of the day's filmstrips and lectures with a new understanding of just how complicated this thing called sex actually was. We left with a long list of worries and concerns, from warts to periods, from pregnancy to impotency. But testosterone won out. Girls were still worth it. Always would be.

Once back together as a gender-mixed class the next morning, the boys and girls avoided each other for a while. It was if we had seen each other naked, and in a way we had. We learned things about each other's bodies that we hadn't known and, in some cases, didn't necessarily want to know. We wouldn't look at each other the same way again. We were speeding toward adulthood, in some ways repulsed, but mostly attracted. But, in either event, it couldn't be stopped. Nor could our rise to adulthood in the church.

So important is the sacrament of confirmation that a bishop administers it. He lays his hands on the candidate and anoints him or her with oil and prayer. The purpose is to encourage the Holy Spirit to strengthen the young person so he or she may lead a more Christlike life. At baptism our parents made the decision to follow Christ on our behalf. But at confirmation we were considered old enough to make the decision for ourselves, with the endorsement of an adult sponsor.

The timing of confirmation could not have been better. It seemed as if the Devil was gaining ground on me. During one episode a week before confirmation, my homeroom teacher Ms. Schmitt turned into an alligator, some of my classmates turned into arrowheads. Animals with nasty bites and Indian stuff were usually my bag, but not when served up this way. I wanted to cry. I wanted help.

I fully expected that confirmation would rid me of the Devil. I had confidence that my standing up for the Lord and inviting the Holy Spirit to come down upon me would melt Satan like a bucket of water did the Wicked Witch of the West. The flame of the Holy Ghost would float *above* my head like it did atop saints pictured on holy cards: a little ball of fire, with a dove hovering nearby.

My classmates and I spent several months in religion classes preparing for confirmation. I took the preparations with the utmost seriousness, afraid that if I somehow messed things up, I would nullify the confirmation, thereby keeping the Devil with me. That's why I carefully crafted the scrapbook we were required to put together prior to confirmation. On the cover of mine I drew a personal coat of arms that included a picture of me crossing the finish line at a track meet, victorious. Included in the scrapbook was a letter I wrote to our pastor:

Dear Father Kennedy, I wish to be confirmed so I can live in Christ and follow in His ways. I hope to take Christ's example with the help of the Holy Spirit. Sincerely, Steve Kissing.

I copied the heartfelt letter off the blackboard. Every other kid in class wrote the same thing. In church, we recited the same prayers, knelt and stood at the same time, and crossed ourselves on command. Everything was carefully scripted. Catholicism was a tidy, orderly faith. Its structure built character and kept one from going astray. God wanted it that way. Among the many pieces of evidence: Noah's Ark. God provided Noah with strict instructions to bring two of every kind of living creature on board. Not three, not four, not a flock or a school or a herd. Two. And only two. Details matter.

I could see no reason why confirmation shouldn't be just as orderly and structured. We did, however, have the freedom to choose our confirmation name, just as our parents had chosen our baptismal names. We could also choose our sponsor, the adult who would stand up for us and pledge to hold us to our commitment, just as our godparents had done at baptism. We were to pick a relative or adult friend whom we admired, an example of good, Christian living.

For my sponsor, I chose my father's younger brother, my Uncle Ken. Like Dad, he was also boyish in appearance though bigger and taller. He drove a VW Bug, too. A purple one. He also shared my father's happy-go-lucky attitude. Uncle Ken and his family, my Aunt Donna and cousins Lisa and Dan, lived in another duplex right around the corner, and Grandma Marge and Grandpa Elmer were the tenants of the first-floor apartment. Our backyards practically touched. Uncle Ken liked to joke around, just like Mom. And he, too, always seemed to be laughing. Uncle Ken would pretend to blow his nose into ten- and twenty-dollar bills and then throw them on the ground as if he didn't care. But as soon as we dove for one of the greenbacks, Uncle Ken would bend over lightning quick and retrieve his cash.

Uncle Ken also went to church. And he kept a statue of the Virgin in his bedroom. A joyful, funny, churchgoing man, Uncle Ken was in my eyes the model Christian.

Another cousin of mine, also named Lisa, the one who lived with her family below our apartment, was in my class and getting confirmed. For her sponsor, she chose my mother. I found the choice a bit odd since my mom didn't practice her faith, at least in the usual ways. On the other hand, Mom was kind-hearted and funny, just like Uncle Ken, so the choice made a lot of sense, too.

For my confirmation name, I chose John, after the Gospel writer St. John the Evangelist. At the request of our teacher, I included a brief biography of St. John in my confirmation scrapbook. I plagiarized a good portion of the bio from an encyclopedia in the school library: "*St. John, the youngest of the Apostles, was called to follow Christ while he was fishing on the Jordan. John was one of the few present during the Transfiguration and the Agony of the Garden. St. John did not deny or run away from his Master at the time of his crucifixion. After Christ's resurrection, John was thrown into a pot of boiling oil. He was miraculously preserved from pain and so reckoned to be a martyr. . . . Later he received heavenly visions.*"

As bad as my situation was, I had not found myself in a pot of boiling oil. At least not yet. I found comfort in St. John's story. I somehow sensed that I, too, would find myself in a steamy cauldron one day. I could only hope that I would be preserved from pain.

The other reason for choosing St. John was to honor my best friend, John "J.C." Callahan. Though Catholic, J.C. attended public school and was a year behind me, so we didn't have the pleasure of getting confirmed together. J.C. and I met when he lived near my home on St. Lawrence just a few doors up from Uncle Ken. By this point, though, J.C.'s family lived about a mile away on Pleasure Drive, also in Price Hill.

J.C. was a wiry kid with brownish blond hair, his blue eyes suggesting he was somewhere else. Despite our close bond, we were something of a yin and yang. I liked school, he didn't. I went to bed early, he stayed up late. He was musical and rhythmic, I couldn't carry a tune or keep a beat. But we had a lot in common, too: strolling around the shopping plaza, climbing trees, and drinking pop by the gallon. Chief among our mutual interests, though, was girls, especially ones starting to "develop."

J.C.'s mother, Ginny, a saint of a woman, was a homemaker. His father, Pat, was a quiet man with a strong presence who worked for the city and also as a part-time bartender at Curnayn's Tavern, one of my Grandpa Elmer's favorite hangouts. Devout Catholics, J.C.'s parents had the genuine, unshakeable religious faith that I wished mine had. Faith that I wished *I* had.

J.C. and I knew our families were strapped for money. There were no elaborate family vacations, fancy cars, or trendsetting wardrobes. But we didn't mind, at least not much. We made do.

On hot summer days we would empty the two thirty-gallon garbage cans behind J.C.'s house, rinse them out, and then fill them with cool water from a hose. We would each sit in one, water up to our chins, the sun in our faces and on our shoulders. We'd talk about school, girls, and the wooded area at the end of Pleasure Drive, where allegedly a naked man, whom some kid dubbed "The Nude Dude," roamed freely like Sasquatch.

I fantasized about how helpful it would be if I could devise a way to fill my garbage can with holy water, maybe even asking J.C. to serve as my John the Baptist, submerging my entire body in the holy fluid. I'd emerge as clean as someone in a soap commercial on the outside and as clean as a saint on the inside.

I told J.C. just about everything. He was the first to know when I liked a certain girl. He was the only person who I'd tell what I confessed in church and what my penance was. But even with best friends there were things best left unsaid. I didn't tell John about how my father behaved at times, though I think J.C. could sense it, largely because we spent considerably more time at his house than mine. I certainly didn't tell J.C. that I thought his younger sister, Sally, was especially cute. Incest was a mortal sin. And I surely didn't tell J.C. about the Devil. It made me wonder what I might not know about J.C. And everyone else in my life. I figured we all had secrets of one sort or another.

After about a half-hour of sitting in the fetal position inside the garbage cans, we'd grow bored. And stiff. We'd rock each other's can until we both tumbled over, water pouring out on to the hot concrete patio, our toes and fingertips wrinkly. We would slip our T-shirts back on and then go about our business, not knowing, or more to the point, not caring, that we smelled like spoiled milk or rotten meat. I have since been to several multimillion gallon waterparks with wave pools, tunnel slides, and meandering canals in which you float aimlessly on an inner tube. But none has even come close to reinvigorating the spirit quite like those garbage cans on Pleasure Drive.

On a mild Thursday evening, we kids of the church walked into St. William, ready to walk out adults—and even more anxious to attend our confirmation parties back home. As mature members of the church we would be expected to leave behind childish ways and more regularly place the needs of others before our own. With the help of the Holy Spirit, I was prepared to do so. Confirmation would not only transform me into an adult, I thought, but completely and totally exorcise my demons in a way that my homespun exorcisms with Wonder Bread had not.

Me, Uncle Ken, Mom, and Cousin Lisa
in front of the Virgin Mary grotto prior
to confirmation.

With parents and family seated inside St. William's—Sisters Lucy, Patricia, and others smiling so big it was as if they could see something interesting or amazing that we didn't—we seventh graders marched in with our sponsors. We wore our finest clothes, the girls in gowns, the boys in suits. I was a bit self-conscious in my grass-green leisure suit trimmed in two rows of white thread. It wasn't the style of the suit that concerned me. I actually thought it looked as good as any. But my mother confessed that she paid only fifteen dollars for it, a small sum for a suit even back in the seventies. I would have felt more confident in my exorcism had my clothes been more expensive. I feared God would be a bit insulted.

The Knights of Columbus, a Catholic men's society, had on hand their honor guard, which consisted of men dressed like musketeers with swords. They marched in behind us, some of the pomp and circumstance called for in light of Bishop August J. Kramer's presence.

We confirmation candidates sang songs, listened to Scripture, and heard some remarks about the responsibility we would soon bear as full members of the church. Then, with camera bulbs flashing, we marched up to be confirmed. I felt strong and certain on the altar. Uncle Ken's hand on my shoulder, Bishop Kramer praying over me, Father Kennedy looking on, smiling.

I was betting everything that by turning my soul completely over to God through confirmation, I would live without demons. No more surprise visits. No more crazy voices. No more headaches.

Hallelujah! Bring on the pot of boiling oil. I will feel no pain!

Back at home for my party, I ate bakery cake with icing as thick as my math textbook. I also opened gifts befitting an adult, Devil-free member of the church: rosaries, religious medals, sweat socks, running shorts, and model rockets.

I had fought fire with fire. The flame of the Holy Spirit was now burning strong above me, extinguishing the Devil's fires within me. I was sure of it.

Chapter 12

Marian Miracles

While I definitely found other girls intriguing, particularly those with the reputations for being quick to make out, associating with such sleazy girls would hasten my demise. As much as I longed to hug an "easy" girl, I couldn't risk giving in to such temptation and give both Jesus and Satan the wrong idea about whose side I was on.

A committed and confirmed soldier of the Lord, I now enjoyed the protection of St. John the Evangelist and the Holy Spirit. My ordeal was over. Jesus: 1. Devil: 0. I grew cocky. I taunted Satan by eating devil's-food cookies and even running on a street that I had heretofore shied away from: Devil's Backbone.

Ha!

My life was coming together.

My running was going well. I won the mile run at the first Catholic school track meet of my seventh-grade season, beating several eighth graders in the process. Eventually some of those

A first-place ribbon that I was certain would irritate Satan.

eighth graders caught up and I had to settle for third or fourth place at most meets that season.

My best mile time that season was 5:25, my best two-mile was 11:29. (Body: ✔+)

My grades were better than ever and one teacher even said that I was among her favorite students. (Mind: ✔+)

My spiritual program included daily prayers, serving Mass three times a week, and going to confession once a month. (Spirit: ✔+).

Near delirious with joy, I awaited an opportunity to tell my family, friends, nuns, and priests about my battle with Satan. I would tell them about how the Devil had been visiting for years, exploiting my weaknesses. I would tell them how I got my act together and fought back alone, brave, determined. I'm not sure that they would have believed me. I'm not sure *I* would have if I were them. But my eyes would tell the truth, I thought. The details would tell the truth. And our faith's core beliefs in evil and redemption would back me up.

But I never got the chance to talk about my spiritual victory. The Devil came back just days after confirmation. And to make matters worse, he

93

visited while I was running, the one time when I felt free of any burden or pressure.

I was gliding along one of my favorite courses. It just so happened to take me past Mother of Mercy High School, where I saw lots of older girls with shapely legs and developed chests. Out of nowhere, the Prince of Darkness decided to set the pace for a while. This route also passed a small office building with a long window against which about ten people had positioned their desks. These pencil pushers often smiled and waved as I ran by effortlessly several days a week, even in May downpours, August heat alerts, and December ice storms.

While running a seven-and-a-half-minute-a-mile pace right in front of this office building, I came to a complete stop within two strides. The office workers had never seen me motionless, and they must not have known what to make of the blank stare I shot back at them. They jumped out of their chairs and pressed their faces against the window. No doubt they were waiting to see if *my* head would do a 360-degree turn.

I didn't see desk jockeys staring back at me but Mary Tyler Moore, my Uncle Lloyd, a zebra, and talking apples. What did it mean? What *could* it mean?

Satan gave my mind back after about ten seconds but it took another twenty seconds or so to get my wits about me, just as one of the office workers, a young man with a look of genuine concern, came outside to check on me. I mumbled "hello" and ran off, leaving him to scratch his head and send a "I'm not sure what just happened" shrug to his colleagues in the window. My head stung with each plant of a foot on the sidewalk.

I avoided running that route for several weeks. That is, until the lure of seeing those Mercy High School girls proved too strong. I just didn't look into that office window anymore, picking up the pace as I ran by. I pulled a similar stunt whenever I worried that someone at school or church caught me staring off into space. I did my best to avoid them for a week or so. This wasn't, of course, always feasible, but I managed it well enough to avoid any meaningful suspicion. In addition, my hyperactive personality and my interest in storytelling—both of which, people must have assumed, required some mental downtime to sustain— provided additional cover.

I cursed my situation. I cursed the Devil. I cursed my cheap, green confirmation leisure suit.

In my never-ending search for an advantage, an ace in the hole, I ended my relationship with Lisa Gruber and instead turned my attention to Mary Ann Farrell. She had expressive green eyes and a soft smile that was cute to the core, like the "Brady Bunch's" Marcia, one groovy chick.

Mary Ann and I didn't talk on the phone. We preferred to keep our sharing to schoolyard chat and, better still, written correspondence. This was good news. I had grown tired of walking to the phone booth and dropping good coins that I otherwise could have used for candy and rocket motors. Mary Ann and I took our writing seriously, sometimes filling more than one side of a notebook page. Mary Ann was a writer, always attentive to details and aiming for the highest of standards. In one letter she wrote, "I apologize for the poor sentence structure."

We decided to go steady at the beginning of eighth grade. This meant I just slid under a critical social deadline. For a boy to lack a girlfriend by eighth grade was to be most uncool and run the serious risk of being labeled an oddball.

Most of the kids in my class were paired up, some formally, meaning that they had actually been seen talking, exchanging letters, or holding hands. Some were paired up informally, meaning that while the two had yet to declare themselves boyfriend and girlfriend, everyone in class knew instinctively that they belonged together. A case in point was Paul Larkin, a nerdy guy who collected Troll dolls, and Margaret McLane, who studied insects on the weekends—just for fun. Weird likes weird, I figured.

The others guys in my class expressed little interest in my Mary Ann. That's because she had three strikes against her. She was quiet. She was a true goodie-two-shoes. And, worst of all, she was tall. Among the tallest kids in class, she had an inch, maybe two, on me. But I didn't care. I would always be looking up to her anyway.

My first real girlfriend was not without fault, though. Her maternal grandmother lived next door to me. That meant that Mary Ann's mom was often right next door taking care of her mother. It also meant that Mary Ann's mom and mine would occasionally spot one another and talk. I hated to see that happen. God only knew what lies my mom was telling Mary Ann's. Whether I was around to witness the two talking or not, Mom would be sure to inform me later.

"Please pass the potatoes," Mom said at dinner once while looking me right in the eyes, even though the potatoes weren't within my reach. "Oh, Stevie, I spoke with Mary Ann's mom this afternoon."

"Great," I said, trying to appear disinterested, while bracing for what was to come.

"She said Mary Ann's in puppy love."

I kept stabbing my meatloaf, pretending it was Mom's tongue. "Great."

"She said *you're* the puppy."

"Great."

"Have you kissed her yet?"

"Just pass one of your delicious frozen fish sticks." I could see Dad and Teri out of the corner of my eye, both snickering.

"Do you hold hands at lunch?" Mom said.

"Yes. And then we have sexual intercourse." Though fighting fire with fire didn't work with Satan, it often did with Mom.

"Stevie! Don't talk like that!"

It was then my turn to snicker.

Certainly Mary Ann's good stature with the Lord would bode well for me, her goodness validating and enhancing what little I had. While I definitely found other girls intriguing, particularly those with the reputations for being quick to make out, associating with such sleazy girls would hasten my demise. As much as I longed to hug an "easy" girl, I couldn't risk giving in to such temptation and give both Jesus and Satan the wrong idea about whose side I was on.

Exactly what Mary Ann saw in me I wasn't sure, and I didn't ask, considering it yet another sleeping dog on the porch of life's many mysteries, kind of like why the nuns never seemed to use the bathroom. (Did they even go?) While I fully expected that Mary Ann's beauty and purity would raise my stock with the Lord and fend off Satan's unwanted advances, I simply ignored the very real possibility that my plan could backfire: Instead of Mary Ann's goodness lifting me toward heaven, my wickedness could drag her down with me to hell. Time would soon tell, though, because I sensed that time was running out.

After three years of wrestling with Satan, his grip on me firm and seemingly constant, I began eighth grade uncertain if I would be sane, or even alive, come graduation. Though it may have been my last year on earth, I longed for the passing of eighth grade with an intensity like no other.

At the end of my final elementary school year, three life-fulfilling events awaited: 1) The Catholic schools track and field championships, in which I intended to win the mile run; 2) The annual eighth-grade talent show, in which I hoped to show off the acting skills that I had honed disguising my demonic condition;

and 3) Graduation itself, the most important part being the dance that followed the ceremony. It was during the dance that I hoped to reap the biggest prize of them all: a girl squished against me.

As I had fully expected, the Devil paid more visits in eighth grade than in the previous years. And even though I had learned to expect a visit at any time, it seemed that when each one came, I was still surprised. I imagined the Devil just waiting for that split second when I dropped my guard before striking, his laugh echoing throughout the dark dungeons of hell, another notch in his pitchfork.

After each episode, it took hours, sometimes days, to feel normal again. But by this point, I wasn't sure I remembered what normal felt like. Though I tried, I could find no rhyme or reason to the timing of Satan's tricks. This was further evidence that something evil was behind my condition. Something more of this world, I assumed, would be more orderly and consistent, easier to nail down.

I refused, however, to give up my search for some pattern in the demonic dementia. I wondered, too, about how I would handle the insanity when it eventually overwhelmed me, as it had seemed to do already with some members of my family and some people in the neighborhood. I brought the topic up one day with Mom.

As she sat at the kitchen table reading her *People* magazine, I inquired about unusual behavior, in and out of the family. For starters, there was Grandpa Elmer. He kept the price sticker on his powder-blue VW Bug for more than five years. He would even sit on plates at restaurants to warm them up. And he soaked his false teeth in bleach, often not bothering to rinse them off before putting them back in, his face a giant pucker. He'd wash the sharp taste down with warm beer.

And then there was Dad's Uncle Herman. He would pretend to call the Easter Bunny—on his hand—every time you saw him.

That made sense when you were four or five, but he kept doing it, even to teenagers. And, weirdest of all, Uncle Herman gave out slices of bread for Halloween one year.

One of the oddest people in the neighborhood was a man who, word had it, enjoyed dressing up in women's clothes. He, too, like Grandpa, Uncle Herman, and Dad, liked the taste of beer.

"Are they crazy?" I asked Mom, searching for an explanation.

"No, just eccentric."

"What's that mean?"

"They like to do things differently than most people."

"What do you mean?"

"Some people are more free-spirited," Mom said with a small chuckle, glancing up from a page with photos of John Travolta and one of the world's best known free-spirits, Elton John.

Just to see how Mom would respond, I wanted to toss Dad into the mix of eccentrics. He did run backwards up steep hills for crying out loud. But I couldn't bring myself to do it. I did, however, ask: "Does drinking have anything to do with how they act?"

"Drinking doesn't help," Mom said with another chuckle. "But drinking doesn't make you nuts."

"So they're not crazy?"

"Nah. Just colorful."

I tried to dance around the topic, push just a bit to see if Mom would say anything else about these people's states of mind—or souls. "I thought it was some sort of brain thing or something."

"Brain thing? No," Mom said, smirking. "But speaking of that, have I told you that you're named after a retarded kid?"

I could tell she wasn't joking. For once. "*What*?" I sat down, my breath taken away. I had never thought to ask why I was named Steve. I assumed my parents weren't feeling particularly creative when they had to name me.

"I chose Stevie because that was the name of this little re-tarded boy in the neighborhood where I grew up," Mom said, with a smile and a glance away. "I used to look after him."

"I didn't know that," I said. What else could I say? Some parents name their kids after saints, presidents, or, at the very least, popular people in the family. Mine named me after some retarded kid. Great. Perhaps that had some affect on me, too.

After talking to Mom, I crossed and double-crossed myself three times and prayed that I would make it through the rest of the school year. Just a couple of months to go at that point. And then I could go bonkers. Die. Whatever.

Mary Ann helped keep me going. She gave me something to live for. I knew she would deliver. And ultimately she did in several important ways.

The righteousness—and the potential spiritual sweepstakes—of my decision to go steady with Mary Ann was confirmed when she was chosen by our teachers to be the May Queen of St. William. This meant she would have the high honor of crowning the Virgin Mary in the May Ceremony—a Catholic tradition in which school children honor Jesus' mother by singing songs such as "Ave Maria." And of course, saying the "Hail Mary" over and over until we'd rather have pencils shoved in our eyes.

The importance of this ceremony cannot be exaggerated. We Catholics are nuts for the Virgin Mary. "Treat her like your own mother," Sister Lucy used to say. In a way I did, once stealing two quarters lying atop the alms box near the Virgin's statue.

To properly prepare for the big afternoon May Crowning ceremony, my entire class suffered through endless practice sessions. Over and over, we marched in and out of church with a military precision befitting the Prince of Peace's mother. And we sang our hearts out like little angels, even though most of us weren't. There was, of course, no question in my case.

Mary Ann walking down the main aisle for
May Crowning.

Mary Ann and her court—another girl and two boys—had a
host of private practice sessions to ensure proper crowning of the
ceramic virgin, rightfully positioned front and center on the altar.
To crown God's mom, Mary Ann, dressed in her ankle-length
gown, would need to climb a small ladder behind the statue. One
misstep and Mary Ann would tumble backward on her butt or,
worse, fall forward, most likely bringing the Mother of God down
with her. I knew the pressure was mounting when Mary Ann
wrote in one of her letters that "all this May Crowning stuff is
making me sick to my stomach." To help ease her anxiety, I said
three extra "Hail Marys" each day.

When May Crowning arrived, we marched solemnly into St.
William, the boys wearing suits and the girls in formal gowns of
every imaginable pastel color. Everyone looked good—even the
dorky guys appeared handsome and the dog-faced girls looked
cute. I chalked this up to some sort of Marian miracle. They were
all around. My Great Aunt Angie, one of my Grandma Marge's

sisters, had a plant that, when it bloomed each year, one could see the Madonna inside it.

Inside St. William for the ceremony, flowers by the hundreds lay at the Blessed Virgin's feet, her white-and-blue ceramic gown as shiny as the jewels in a chalice. Every candle on or near the altar was lit. And light from the stained-glass windows poured down on the pews, making it look like each person standing or kneeling in the beams of light had a colored halo.

Mary Ann, looking as good as Farah Fawcett, beamed brighter and more wonderful than the Virgin herself. I felt guilty for feeling this way, but I believed it was true. Mary Ann's beauty and purity made her the perfect choice, I thought, to venerate the Virgin and, in so doing, sock it to Satan.

After a half-hour of incense, hymns, and Bible readings, everyone in the standing-room-only crowd watched my Mary Ann climb the ladder without the slightest tremble. She placed the floral crown on the Virgin, camera bulbs flashing, the organ heaving, stained glass light dancing. Never had I seen so many rosary beads being worked over at once.

Knowing that the sweet and pretty Mary Ann—so full of grace and the Lord with thee—had pledged her love to me, I smiled like a kid who had just gotten a raise in his allowance. With Mary Ann at my side, I hoped to forestall forever the day when I, too, would soak dentures in bleach and pass out slices of bread for Halloween.

Chapter 13

A Trophy Life

I wanted to one-up Mom. And spite Satan. The penis-freezing weather he cooked up was not enough to stop me. I decided to run 405 laps, three miles—one each for the Father, Son, and Holy Spirit.

I had no doubt that Jesus was delighted with how well I cared for my body. I was only fourteen years old but capable of running endless miles. I viewed my daily run as something of a prayer, a way of praising God with my feet, legs, lungs, and, most importantly, my heart. And since the Devil had only visited me once while running, I found additional solace in the strenuous exercise. The daily pounding of pavement toughened my body and helped me develop a tolerance for pain that I was certain would come in handy when the Devil would really put the screws to me.

By the end of eighth grade, I had amassed a streak of longer than a year without missing a day of training. My idol was England's Ron Hill, the winner of the 1970 Boston Marathon, whose training streak stretched back to December 1964. And he was still adding to it. Such commitment as Hill and I exhibited certainly pleased the Lord and disappointed Satan, so I let nothing interfere with my daily run, each check mark on the calendar a sign of my resolve.

I ran when sick, when tired, even with intestinal distress, once having to make a dash for a plot of woods to keep from spoiling my shorts. How empowering to know that no illness, no amount of homework, no offer to play after school could stand in my way.

But keeping the streak alive required remarkable measures at times, as the Devil put many an obstacle in my path, Mom chief among them.

One morning, my siblings and I sat quietly at the kitchen table, eating our oatmeal and listening to the radio. We hoped to hear our schools mentioned yet again in the roll call of those closed by the blizzards marking the harsh winters of that era. It was so bitterly cold during those years that the Ohio River—which meandered around the base of Price Hill—turned icy and froze over. The wind occasionally blew the temperature down to 50 below zero, enough, teachers and TV weathermen constantly warned us, to kill a naked person in less than two minutes. This meant sure death for the Nude Dude, the Sasquatch guy in the woods.

For me, the unusually fierce winters were meteorological evidence that these were indeed troubled times, that the Antichrist was up to no good. Intense heat in my head, bone-chilling cold outside. Such extreme opposites coexisting was an omen. I remembered learning as a young child that whenever it rained while the sun was shining meant that the Devil was getting married.

But even winds that could suck the life out of a naked, warm-blooded creature in mere minutes would not prevent me from keeping my running streak alive. Mom, however, was an entirely different matter.

An hour after rejoicing with my sister and brothers for yet another snow day, I stood in the hallway near the living room, forcing a zipper up on a purple warm-up jacket I stretched over two long-sleeved T-shirts and two sweatshirts. My legs were difficult to bend, constricted by a pair of long underwear, my purple warm-up pants, and a gray pair of sweatpants over them. I wore extra-thick wool socks and not one, but two cotton-knit hats. I was ready to run in Antarctica.

I also shoved two small towels down my underwear to protect my genitals. I couldn't be too careful. Word was spreading around school about several unfortunate men in town—one even the cousin of another kid's next-door neighbor's boss's brother-in-law—who got frostbite on their penises. They had to be amputated. Without anesthesia.

My cursing the stubborn zipper on my warm-up jacket caught Mom's attention. "What are you doing?" she asked, as if she didn't know.

"Going bowling," I said laughing, trying to bend over to tie my shoe.

"Over my dead body. You'll die out there!"

"A little snow and wind ain't going to kill me," I said, finally down on one knee. "I'll be back in less than twenty minutes."

"No."

"Ten minutes. I'll be back in *ten* minutes."

"No."

I tried to remain calm. Rational. I stood up. Slowly. "I'll stay close."

"I said 'no.' Absolutely not. No, no, no, no, NO." Mom had that look about her, at once tough and not to be messed with yet also sort of sensitive and teary. I hated that look, as it meant she was sure to win.

"I'll just jog around the block a couple of times," I said, trying to give my best sensitive and teary look. "I'll stay close. I swear!"

"You bet you will; you're not going anywhere!"

"I've got to keep my streak alive."

"I don't care about your damn streak. It's *you* I want alive." Mom positioned herself between me and the stairs leading down and out.

"Please. I'll be back in just five minutes."

"Your lungs will freeze."

"I'll be fine. C'mon. Please. *Please!*"

"Forget it, Stevie. We're not talking about this any more." Mom gave me a slight push toward the stairs leading *up* to my bedroom. I decided to do my begging before someone who would understand. "Dad! Dad!"

Dad was home, his office, like virtually all of the others around town, also closed for the day. As a fellow runner, Dad would understand. He would explain things to Mom. Maybe he'd even run with me. Unfortunately, though, even his pleas didn't sway her. I stormed upstairs to my room, first to sulk, then to wonder whether Olympian Ron Hill had an overbearing mother, and, finally, to plot my escape. I would pay the consequences later, perhaps no TV for a week. Or two. But I decided to risk it anyway.

All I had to do was sneak outside and start running. No one in the family was capable of catching me on foot, of course. Even Dad's quick speed was no match for me if I had a head start. And the Beige Bomber was buried under two feet of wet snow at the end of our driveway-turned-skating-rink.

I figured the best thing would be to sneak out through the basement door. I wasn't sure, though, whether I'd be able to open it without causing some commotion. Odds were, snow and ice had frozen it shut. I tiptoed down the stairs to investigate, but as soon as I made it to our unfinished basement, an option came to mind. There was a way for me to get in my run while avoiding *any* risk of punishment.

I bounced back up the stairs three at a time to retrieve a yardstick and a calculator. I then returned to the basement and measured the distance from the southern wall to the northern. A virtual authority on the traditional high school cinder track, I knew that one lap, 440 yards, was equivalent to a quarter mile. Therefore, 4 x 440, or 1760 yards, equaled a mile. For the first time, I applied math skills to something truly worthwhile. I calculated that I had to run 135 "laps" for each mile. Two miles, or 270 laps, would be enough to meet my daily minimum requirement.

But I wanted to one-up Mom. And spite Satan. The penis-freezing weather he cooked up was not enough to stop me. I decided to run 405 laps, three miles—one each for the Father, Son, and Holy Spirit.

I ran back upstairs and announced my intentions in a snotty tone, loud enough for Mom to hear. I then promptly returned to the basement, this time in just one long-sleeved T-shirt, shorts minus the genital-protecting towels, and warm-up pants sans long underwear.

Ping-ponging from wall to wall, I felt prouder about myself with each touch of our home's frozen foundation. Everyone in my family—even Mom—came down to watch for a couple of minutes before the chill sent them retreating back upstairs, laughing and shaking their heads. I interpreted their delight and dismay as a sign of my endurance, both physical and mental. Jesus was smiling, too; the Devil, no doubt, frowning. He sent a mean blizzard and a stubborn mother to foil my plans. That day, however, I turned a cold shoulder to them both.

It occurred to me while showering after my 405 dizzying laps that had I lived in a home with a paneled basement and pool tables, I likely would not have had the room to run. That day shed new meaning on the phrase, "Blessed are the poor."

My commitment to training paid off on the track. I participated in one race in which the contestants were given one hour to see how far they could run. I covered nine miles and six hundred yards, placing fourth overall, beating people in their twenties and thirties. Having won the four races leading up to the Catholic schools championship meet in May, I was favored to win the mile run. But Jimmy Klunk, my chief competition from nearby St. Ignatius School, had been gaining on me throughout the season.

Besides, anything can happen in a mile-long race. Muscle cramps. A tumble. And the fear of fears: diarrhea. About a year prior, I had made the mistake of drinking some apple juice before a five-mile road race. I spent more time in the Port-a-Pottys alongside the course than I actually did running it, cursing my colon with every stride.

The morning of the championship meet, I ate only two slices of bread, and then, in the stairway leading to my bedroom, I uttered a special collection of prayers I strung together and called the Grand Trilogy: three "Our Fathers," three "Hail Marys," and three "Glory Be's." The concoction was spiritual dynamite.

I then put on my uniform, an ensemble I had assembled myself. I was the only member of the St. William's track team that year, and so the school had even less of a reason to bother with uniforms. Undaunted, I had planned my own for months with the same creative intensity that I imagined Liberace did in designing his concert outfits. I wanted to sparkle, figuratively and literally. And I wanted to intimidate my competitors, just as those kids from the paneled-basement parishes in their shiny nylon uniforms had done. After considering dozens of possibilities, I settled on yellow-striped tube socks, yellow running shorts, and a dark-blue T-shirt with "St. William's Track" emblazoned across my chest in metallic, rainbow-colored, iron-on letters.

I vowed to make St. William the toast of the championship meet by winning track-and-field's premier event—the mile run.

While the first-place finishers of the other events received ribbons, the victor in the mile ran away with a trophy. I watched the trophy handed to last year's victor and fantasized about that moment all year.

I entered the Roger Bacon High School stadium that Sunday afternoon eager to race, my uniform hidden under my purple warm-up suit. My plan was to dazzle everyone when I finally walked onto the cinder track. To loosen up, I did some jumping jacks and toe-touches. I then took a mile-long warm-up jog away from the stadium so as to be able to make a grand entrance at the right time.

While warming up, I uttered the Grand Trilogy again, just for good measure. I did several wind sprints and then heard my call to the start line. I stripped off my warm-up suit and handed it to Dad. Mom winked at me. I then ran onto the track in a blaze of St. William's blue and gold. Some of my competitors blinked in amazement while a few giggled and sneered, a nervous reaction, no doubt. The race was over before it even began, I thought. They just should have handed me the trophy. *My* trophy.

When the gun went off, I shot to the lead and didn't look back. I paid no attention to my dozen competitors or to the crowd of several hundred spectators. Instead, I entertained visions of holding the trophy, its marble base solid in my hand, the gold-plated metal glistening in the sun as I raised it above my Devil-free head. I didn't care how fast, or slow, I ran the race, just as long as I won it. And the trophy.

Although I didn't know it, going into the fourth and final lap, I had a real chance of running the mile in under five minutes, something no Catholic elementary school boy in town had ever done. It was my chance to be something of a Jim Ryun, the guy who broke the four-minute barrier as a high school student. I ran the race, as was my typical custom, without my glasses. So I squinted the whole way, giving some the false impression that I was smiling, with plenty of energy in reserves. But the truth was that I was hurting—and too afraid to look back.

I was also too fatigued to hear the stadium announcer who, I learned later, had begun shouting into his microphone. "Kissing is solidly in the lead and could break the historic five-minute barrier. . . . He has 220 yards to go and is going to have to kick it in to break five minutes. . . . Kissing has 100 yards to go and he just may do it . . . 4:57, 4:58, 4:59, 5 minutes. No, not this time, folks, but he does finish in a very respectable 5:04, 5:05 . . . clock it at 5:07. Just two seconds shy of the city record."

As my competitors finished the race—Jimmy Klunk, the second-place finisher, was more than ten seconds behind—I caught my breath and then strolled around in front of the stands, accepting congratulations, my uniform twinkling in the sunshine.

All the talk in the stands was about how close I came to breaking the city record and the daunting five-minute barrier. Dad thought that if someone were tighter on my heels, I would have been pushed to the record. Mom suggested that, had she cut my Afro—the hairstyle I had been wearing for a couple of years that had become my trademark—I could have shaved seconds off my time. "Too much wind resistance, 'Fro boy," she said. She was probably right. I didn't care much, though. I just wanted that gorgeous trophy.

My hard work, daily runs, and earnest prayers had paid off. The Devil had been coming on strong, but I doubted that even he could run a near-five-minute mile. I was called to the infield for the awards ceremony to receive my trophy, to earn more of the crowd's admiration, and to shake the hands of my competitors who had just eaten my cinder dust. A race volunteer handed Greg Finelli his third-place ribbon and patted him on the back. He then shook Jimmy Klunk's hand and gave him his second-place ribbon. He then grinned ear to ear and handed me my first-place . . . ribbon? "This is the mile-run ceremony," I whispered, not wanting to embarrass him or seem less than gracious. "The winner gets a trophy." I cut the guy some slack, an obvious first-timer who was unaware of the hallowed traditions that have shaped this meet for at least three years, maybe more.

"Not this year, son, we had to cut back on the budget. Sorry," he said, handing me my ribbon. I couldn't believe it. I had been training my butt off all year to win a trophy, something big and bulky and shiny, something with demon-stopping power. I stormed over to Mom and Dad, who were off to the side, smiling and giving me the thumbs up. I announced that I was ready to leave. *Now*.

On the ride home, I stared out the back window of the Beige Bomber, my tongue pinched between my teeth, my chintzy ribbon shoved in one of my sweaty spikes, the same place I put my parents' congratulations. The Devil had screwed me, I thought, but I dared not say it. Without the trophy, Jesus was surely less impressed, too.

The very next day, the Devil paid a visit as I sat at the dining room table writing answers to the questions at the end of my history chapter. Had that trophy been in the house, the Devil would not have come. I put the rest of my homework off until the morning. Later, lying in bed, my head still hurting, I cursed—three times—my predicament and that damn-ribbon-that-should-have-been-a-trophy.

Chapter 14

Let 'Em In

I definitely knew what it was like to have something go suddenly and unexpectedly bad. All of life's unpredictability made me angry at times. I just wanted the world to be neater, tidier. But as with my own bedroom, I wanted someone else to do the cleaning.

Way back in second grade when my reading class decided to put on a play about Paul Bunyan, I volunteered to accept the role no one wanted: Babe the Blue Ox. I wore blue sweatpants, a blue hooded sweatshirt, and blue papier-mâché horns. I crawled around on all fours carefully delivering my lines, each a grunt or a snort. After the play, my teacher said that I should expect a call from Hollywood the next time they needed a blue ox. The other kids were green with envy.

In third grade, at Mom's suggestion, I dressed up like a woman for a school Halloween contest. Putting on her pantyhose sent a weird, yet pleasurable, tingle up my spine. This alarmed me. I buried the thought deep in my mind, the same place I would later put the memories of the murdered gerbils. The mental anguish was worth it, though, because I came in third place and won a candy bar, which I promptly put in my purse.

Given all the acting required to hide my demonic condition, by eighth grade I came to appreciate any and all opportunities to show off my performing skills—and to keep them super-sharp. I figured that pretending everything was okay was only going to become an increasingly difficult proposition.

J.C. and I played explorer in the woods near his home. He was usually Daniel Boone or Geronimo, and I was Tecumseh or Davy Crockett. Sometimes we were the Totem Pole Spies, a gang we created and of which we were the only members. I even made official membership cards with Dad's typewriter paper, colored markers, and clear plastic Mom bought to cover the furniture. As we hiked through the woods, J.C. and I kept a lookout for bears, hostile Indian tribes, and, of course, the Nude Dude.

I played space travelers with a number of pals, including Rick Lenihan, a kid from Indiana who spent his summers with his grandparents who lived around the corner from us. We would pretend that one of our backyards was the surface of a remote planet in a distant universe. My bushy hair and Rick's hands, badly deformed at birth, gave each of us something of an alien appearance.

Usually at some point in the space fantasies, I would drop to my knees, hands around my neck, shouting, "The atmosphere! The at-mos-phere! The at-mooos-pheeerrre! The at . . . " I'd then collapse on the ground and Rick would revive me with the help of squirt gun that also served as a nuclear-powered medical device.

And I played rock star—all by myself. When no one was around, I would spin one of my brother's albums in our bedroom, sometimes playing my "guitar," actually my mother's broom, and sometimes lip-synching into an empty toilet paper roll.

Elton John's ballads, such as "Daniel" and "Don't Let the Sun Go Down on Me," were especially good for creating an emotional connection with my arena full of crying, screaming fans—all girls, each of whom was tossing her bra and panties at my feet. Peter Frampton's tunes, especially "Do You Feel Like We Do," helped me show off my awesome guitar skills. And vintage Chicago allowed me to play the trumpet while looking cool and not like some dork in a marching band.

By far my favorite rock star to impersonate was Paul McCartney. The throngs of people in my bedroom arena simply adored me when I lip-synched such classics as "Jet," "Band on the Run," and "Junior's Farm."

My fascination with McCartney was driven in part by my brother Larry's love for him and the Beatles. I was beside myself with envy when Larry was permitted to go to the "Wings Over America" tour when it made its Cincinnati stop at Riverfront Coliseum. I begged Mom and Dad to let me go, but they would have none of it.

"You're too young, Stevie," Mom told me. "I don't want you mixing with that crowd. They'll be plenty of hooligans."

"But it's okay for Larry to mix with them?" I asked, somehow thinking that by questioning Mom's judgement she would allow me to go.

"He's older and knows a hooligan when he sees one."

"Well, then, he can protect me."

"He doesn't want you with him."

I knew she was right. Besides, I didn't have a ticket. I tried to win some from radio stations who had call-in contests. But all I ever got were busy signals. The Devil was no doubt jamming the line.

On the day of the show, Larry and a friend, Matt, left before sunup to be among the first in line. They brought along a radio, a deck of cards, some magazines, and a Styrofoam cooler with drinks and sandwiches.

I spent the day playing my brother's McCartney albums. Fueled in part by my disappointment over not being able to go, my bedroom concerts that day were the most energetic to date. I even threw in a couple of guitar smashes. It was the only time I can recall actually taking a broom to my bedroom's hardwood floor.

I did my best to stay up until Larry got home. I wanted to hear *every* detail about the concert: the playlist, the wardrobes, the light show.

Despite my best efforts, I was asleep by ten o'clock, no doubt worn out by all the dancing, jumping, and guitar strumming on my stage. I did, however, perk right up a few hours later when Larry shuffled into the room.

"So, how was it?" I asked. "How did it go? Was it cool? Was it? How were your seats?"

Larry mumbled something back, but I couldn't understand it. "What?"

He mumbled something else again.

"*What?*" I said. "I can't hear you."

This time I heard him loud and clear. "Shut up. I'll tell you tomorrow."

"Why?"

"There were problems. Go back to bed."

"Problems? What kinds of problems? Didn't he show up? Did the power go out?"

"Go to fucking sleep," Larry said. He never talked liked that, at least to me. He took off his clothes and lay in bed. I couldn't believe that he wasn't coughing up the details. I wondered if Larry got some drugs off a hooligan.

"What are you talking about?" I said, still hoping Larry would toss me a bone of some sort.

"I thought I was going to die. Okay? *That's* the story." He then rolled over, leaving me to wonder just what may have happened. I found out the next morning.

As it turned out, Larry and Matt were among the first in line. By the early evening, and before the doors were open, a massive crowd had gathered behind them at Riverfront Coliseum. The crowd started to push forward, putting considerable pressure on those near the front. There were points when Larry and Matt were squeezed with such force that they had trouble breathing. They even feared that they may be pushed through the doors, no doubt sliced to death by the shattered glass.

The experience was so traumatic that it prevented Larry and his friend from really enjoying the concert, something they had been looking forward to for months. What was supposed to have been a very big day turned out to be one of Larry's worst. I could relate. I definitely knew what it was like to have something go suddenly and unexpectedly bad. All of life's unpredictability made me angry at times. I just wanted the world to be neater, tidier. But as with my own bedroom, I wanted someone else to do the cleaning.

So scared, agitated, and disappointed by what happened, Larry and Matt wrote a letter to city hall, suggesting big problems were going to happen if things didn't change with crowd management.

Their letter—and warnings of all sorts from others—didn't make it to the right people. Or, if they did, the messages didn't make it through their thick skulls.

Months later The Who came to town. Another crowd gathered and began to push forward. Many people had their breath taken away. Eleven never got it back.

Of course, it occurred to me that had the same thing happened at the McCartney & Wings concert, it could have been my brother who was squeezed to death. I felt bad for those who lost their brothers and sisters, sons and daughters. But I felt even worse for myself. Mom was *never* going to let me go to a concert.

The news of the Who tragedy spooked us all. Rock and roll was supposed to be fun, energetic, and full of life. But on that day it was about nothing other than fear and death.

The DJ's played a lot of Who songs, especially "The Song Is Over." Some people created memorials for the dead near the arena, little shrines made of candles, flowers, and Who album covers. Some of the burn-outs in the neighborhood, the kids with an extra fondness for hard rock music and cigarettes and a distaste for schoolwork and sports, wore black armbands with their black concert T-shirts.

I found my own way to honor the fallen rock fans. During a bedroom concert, I dedicated a particularly heartfelt rendition of McCartney's "Let 'Em In" to the Who victims.

Another entertainment-themed, community-wide tragedy of my youth was the big fire at the Beverly Hills Supper Club in Northern Kentucky, right across the Ohio River. It was, I had been told, one of the swankiest places in town. I envisioned rich people driving up in Cadillacs and then stepping out wearing tuxedoes and formal gowns, gold and diamond jewelry on their hands and around their necks, exotic furs on their shoulders.

My parents once won a raffle and went to the Beverly Hills Supper Club to see Lou Rawls perform. Luckily their swanky night out missed the evening of the tragedy, but hundreds of others were not so fortunate. They came for fine dining and to listen to entertainer John Davidson. A spark caused by faulty wiring started a blaze that spread quicker than a dirty joke at school. Panic ensued. Scores of people died.

I received word of the fire the next morning when I showed up at church where I sold *Cincinnati Enquirer*s to parishioners as they left Mass. Banner headlines awaited me: "120 Feared Dead, Scores Hurt as Beverly Hills Club Blazes." I sold out of newspapers after just one Mass; it usually took three.

After Mass, Father Kennedy spent a few minutes chatting with me as he often did. He said that he was returning from some event the night before and he saw the sky all ablaze. He knew something horrible was happening.

"I've got to believe that something good will come of this," he said, as he held one of my papers, shook his head, and crossed himself.

I had no clue what good could come of all that death. Eventually the body count would rise to 165. But I was sure something could because Father Kennedy seemed absolutely certain.

Despite the dangers of performing, I forged on. Every day was something of an act for me, though there were no standing ovations. My acting abilities were rewarded with silence, just the way I wanted it. But some real applause would also be a good thing, I thought. So I eagerly signed up to perform in the eighth grade talent show, an annual tradition at St. William.

My buddy Lane Froelich and I decided to entertain with kazoos—the only instrument that I could *really* play—and tell jokes. We lifted most of them from comedy books and albums. I thought our material would provide much needed comic relief for the other acts, which included two guys doing the Abbott & Costello bit "Who's on First?" That was an inane routine, if you asked me, perhaps still bitter over my own disastrous Little League career.

After nearly a month of practices during every music class, the big day arrived. We eighth graders would perform our songs and skits for the rest of the school that afternoon and then, that night, repeat the show for our parents and other parishioners.

Lane and my act fell flat with the rest of the school. We were humiliated. And we were prepared to toss in the towel—and our kazoos—rather than suffer more embarrassment before the entire parish. We licked our wounds in the classroom-turned-dressing room near the stage.

Thankfully, though, one of our teachers talked us out of early show biz retirement. "Those kids were just too young to appreciate your humor," she told us. "You guys are born comedians."

That made sense to us. Our finely honed—if plagiarized—act was too sophisticated for a group of runny-nosed peons. We decided to forge on. We would hop on stage that night, kazoos in hand, deliberately baggy suits hanging off our bodies, as thin as Don Knotts'.

As planned, we appeared on stage three times. We opened with a bang.

"Knock, knock," I said to the crowd.

"Who's there," a couple hundred people responded.

"Sam and Janet," Lane said.

"Sam and Janet *who*?" the crowd asked.

We belted out the punch line: "Sam and Janet evening." A wave of laughter washed over us. I couldn't recall ever feeling better.

We concluded our third and final set with another crowd pleaser:

"Have you heard about the one-armed fisherman?" I asked the crowd, pointing to Lane, a few feet away. He kept one arm behind his back, the other at his side.

"No!" they shouted back.

Lane pulled out *one* arm and extended it fully.

"He caught a fish that big," I said. The crowd laughed as if I was Bob Hope and Lane was Paul Lynde.

Our teacher was right. We *were* funny.

Of course, all of my admiring fans had only a glimpse of my true acting talents. My best performances were yet to come.

Chapter 15

Dance Lessons

I felt safe with this godly girl, so beautiful, so bright, so beatified. The Devil was no doubt pissed that I could attract a girl of such stature. He wanted me with a slut, but I danced with a saint. And the saint led, for this sinner had no rhythm and, at the moment, he wanted to go wherever this goddess was willing to take him.

The Devil had come on strong in the final weeks of eighth grade, taunting me, keeping me on my toes to the very end. He even paid a visit at the beauty parlor where Mom worked and where I usually got my trademark Afro perms.

My classmates had forgotten that my hair was, back in sixth grade, as straight as the lines we drew with our protractors in math class. Everyone came to believe that my bushy, "Mod Squad" mop, broad enough to eclipse the sun, was as natural as the trees. But it was no more real than the breasts some girls allegedly manufactured from wadded-up tissues.

It took my mom, a certified beautician, nearly an hour to wrap more than seventy small curlers in my hair. And another hour or so to apply the chemicals and supervise the drying and rinsing. Whether at home or the beauty parlor, the perm procedure provided Mom and me a chance to bond every couple of months. Dad and I had our running; Mom and I had our perming. I wouldn't swap either experience for the world.

I did my best to sit still while Mom secured curlers to my head or trimmed my hair. She would quiz me about school, J.C. and other friends, and, of course, girls. I answered all but the girl questions. Mom always gave me money for a bottle of pop or two, and she usually had candy at her station. When she didn't, she would send me with some of her tip money to a nearby bakery. I'd come back with some cherry turnovers and genuine gratitude that Mom hankered for sugar as much as I did.

My head doused with multiple bottles of pungent chemicals, I sat next to old ladies talking about grocery store bargains and upcoming flea markets. The worst part, though, was sitting still under the hair dryer dome. The heat and chemicals made my head itch worse than an arm inside a cast in mid-August.

While I suffered through this beauty shop torture a week before graduation, the Devil came to say hello. How apropos, I thought later, the burning, stinking chemicals on my head and the hot air in my face no doubt a hint of hell itself. My head felt as if it were shoved up a jet engine rather than a hair dryer. Shortly after the visit, when Mom was applying another chemical to my head, she bragged about my talent show performance to one of her customers. I forced a smile when the old lady said, "Sounds like you have a bright future ahead of you." At that moment, I really didn't think so.

Perming my hair presented two significant risks. First, if I were ever spotted by one of my classmates in a beauty parlor with pink and baby blue curlers in my hair, my life would be over—in an instant. Death by humiliation.

Second, to ensure that the new do set properly, I couldn't wash my hair for several days after the perm. I had to walk around smelling like a large permanent marker with its cap off, the stench enough to bring tears to people's eyes. This is why I preferred to get coiffed on Saturdays. The worst of the smell would dissipate before I returned to school on Monday. With a fresh perm tightening my curls, my classmates just assumed that I had gotten my hair cut, which did, in fact, precede every perm.

The 'Fro risks were worth it, though. A head full of curls worked for Juan Epstein on *Welcome Back, Kotter* and for Greg Brady on *The Brady Bunch*. It would help me with the ladies, too. My life seemed ruled by lies, those I wore on the top of my head and those I carried within it. But at least I looked good. Or so I thought.

And at no point did looking good matter as much as graduation. From the moment I woke up that day, I could think only of what was waiting for me after the ceremony in the church undercroft. For the first time, I would dance with a real live girl. Actually, it was to be the second time.

The day before, overcome with anxiety that I would be the only boy who didn't know how to slow dance, I broke down and asked Mom for a lesson. She stepped away from the ironing board in our dining room, "It's So Easy" by Linda Ronstadt playing on the little hi-fi behind us. "Put your hands here like this," Mom said, as she tugged my arms from their sides and put them around her waist. "And then *Mary Ann* will . . . "

"*Mo-omm!*"

"I mean, *I* will, put my arms around you like this," she said, draping her arms over my shoulders. "And then you move to the music like this."

"Okay! Okay! I get it," I said, stepping away from Mom, the mere thought of her as even a surrogate girlfriend grossing me out. I would have to make do with the two-second, two-sway lesson.

The next day, with my locks wound as tight as I was, I strutted into church with my classmates for graduation Mass. The flash of cameras was outdone only by the smiles of proud parents in the pews. I was one of several students asked to read at the Mass. I read the intercessions, the prayers making a request of God. Among the seven intercessions was: "That, like Christ, we may grow in wisdom, age, and grace before God and man."

How pleased I was to have made it through eighth grade! And how I hoped that I would continue to grow in age, if not wisdom and grace. The joy of finishing elementary school, the thought of going on to high school, particularly one with a superb cross-country program, combined with the opportunity to rub up against a girl made my head spin. Graduation Mass seemed to drag, in part because I expected the Devil to visit and ruin the biggest day of my life. I crossed and double-crossed myself so many times that I lost count.

After the Mass, which Satan did not interrupt, my classmates and I suffered through endless hugs and kisses from parents and grandparents. One by one we escaped and high-tailed it down to the undercroft for the real commencement ceremony. The undercroft was a large bi-level room with a linoleum floor and primary-colored carpet panels on the walls.

The dance would be the last time we'd all be together as a class. While most of us were headed to a Catholic high school in the fall, more than a few were going to public schools where mostly Protestants and nonbelievers went. The one thousand-dollar-a-year tuition fee at the Catholic high schools was hard on most of our parents. And out of the question for some.

Although throughout the year we ridiculed whatever weakness we could spot in one another—Greg Johnson's tendency to stutter, Mary Windmer's eyes, one blue, one gray—we had also grown to accept one another at some deeper level. Despite our shortcomings and the difference in brains, beauty, and brawn, we were all equals that night. Not one person was teased for being too fat, too tall, or too skinny. Too dumb, too ugly, or too hairy. Together we survived mushy nuns, long division, and worse, horrific photos of war and genital warts. It was a night to celebrate if there ever was one.

The girls danced by themselves while we guys hung out in the back near the punch and snacks, trying to look cool and hide the fact that we were all about to wet our pants. With prodding from the adult chaperones, a few boys, myself included, walked to the edge of the dance floor. We rocked stiffly back and forth, snapping our fingers to the Commodores' "Brick House."

And then it happened—the first slow dance of the night, Orleans' "Dance with Me." I fantasized all year about that moment. Yet I wished I had another year to prepare. *Why didn't I spend more time with Mom getting a proper lesson or two? Do I keep my hand on Mary Ann's hips or on her back? What if she expects me to dance with one arm out like Fred Astaire? Oh Jesus, I just want to go home!*

As the song began, the girls approached the boys. My mouth was dry, despite the gallon of punch I swallowed in the past fifteen minutes. I turned to walk away. But Mary Ann cut me off at the pass. "Would you like to dance?" she asked.

"Yeah, sure." We walked to the center of the dance floor. I put my arms around her waist. She slid her arms around my neck. The softness of her hands and the silkiness of her dress made me shiver. I felt safe with this godly girl, so beautiful, so bright, so beatified. The Devil was no doubt pissed that I could attract a girl of such stature. He wanted me with a slut, but I danced with a saint. And the saint led, for this sinner had no rhythm and, at the moment, he wanted to go wherever this goddess was willing to take him.

"You look nice," Mary Ann said.

"You . . . look . . . great . . . too," I said, having to concentrate on every word as if I was speaking a foreign tongue.

"Thanks. Can you believe we graduated?"

"No, it came so fast. How about you?" I sounded even more stupid than I did on the radio that one day, but I didn't know what else to say.

"Yes, it came fast," Mary Ann said, her warm breath on my neck. "Are your parents throwing you a party?"

"Yes, tomorrow. How about you?"

"Sunday afternoon. What are you getting?"

"Some clothes and some running shoes. How about you?"

"Clothes and a pair of roller skates."

In my mind I saw myself running down the street in my new Nikes, Mary Ann skating alongside me, pacing me, occasionally getting out ahead of me where I could see her nice butt.

"Are you getting a family pass to the pool this summer?"

"Yeah. How about you?"

"Yes. Yes, we are."

We being a man and woman of letters, that was one of the longest conversations we had all year. I didn't know what else to say, and I didn't want to talk anyway. I smelled her perfume, which was not mediciney like some teachers' or overpowering like the sluts'. No, Mary Ann smelled the way I imagined Hawaii did, floral with a hint of a fresh breeze. I concentrated on the last social studies lesson I could recall—"The Mayan Indians built temples to honor the sun god, Ra"—trying to keep myself from getting too aroused. The Devil was trying to spoil the moment. A big woody now would certainly repulse the love of my life and splinter our relationship. The slow song ended and the DJ picked the beat up again, this time with KC and the Sunshine Band's "Shake Your Booty."

The burden of the first slow dance off our shoulders, we guys loosened up. Most of us stayed on the dance floor with the girls. They danced gracefully, while we boys twisted and contorted like monkeys with severe arthritis. But we didn't care, and the girls didn't seem to mind, either.

And now I see how that graduation dance so perfectly captured my predicament. While I enjoyed physical pleasures in the undercroft, above me was the church, the heavenly world, where I was but an hour ago. And so I spent my days balancing between the two worlds, too afraid to let go of what was upstairs, most unwilling to detach from what was downstairs.

With elementary school behind us and a long summer ahead of us, we graduates danced the rest of the night—both fast and slow—without a single care or concern. Of course we were too young and naïve to know that we would never dance that way again. And I couldn't know that within the course of a couple of weeks my gorgeous, saintly Mary Ann, the May Queen, would take me to heaven. And to hell.

Throughout eighth grade I begged God for survival until the end of the school year. My prayers did not fall on deaf years. And along the way, I had won the Catholic schools mile run, soaked up audience approval at the talent show, and danced cheek-to-cheek with an angel. I thought I would be ready to end my battle with Satan, toss my hands up, and let the cards fall where they may. But the events of the preceding nine months had not left me with a sense of fulfillment. Instead, I longed for more. More first-place finishes. More applause. And, most definitely, more slow dances.

Maybe in another year or so I would have been ready to lie down and die. Or go berserk. But definitely not at this point, not with a summer lying out before me with all its treats and temptations.

I decided to fight on.

As elementary school graduates, my friends and I were afforded certain privileges. Most notably, we could stay out later on Friday and Saturday nights. This meant more time to hang on corners, cruise parish festivals, and attend dances.

Exactly one week after my graduation, J.C. and I walked to St. Lawrence's party hall for our first Catholic Youth Organization (CYO) dance. Each of us sported a carefully chosen wardrobe. He wore gray corduroys and a handsome, sky-blue, terry cloth shirt with a large zipper down the front. I wore blue corduroys and a plaid shirt ablaze with primary colors, one of my graduation gifts. I spent a half-hour shaping my 'Fro into a perfectly round ball of fur.

As we walked to St. Lawrence, I worked my 'Fro over with a plastic pick in an unsuccessful attempt to counteract wind damage. Inside the school's cafeteria/bingo hall, I noticed that the lights were dimmed, which I liked. But virtually everyone in attendance was a high school student, which I didn't like. There were girls with big chests, which I liked. But boys with bulging muscles and facial hair, which I didn't like.

It hit me then that I was no longer competing with my grade school classmates for Mary Ann's heart. She was now in a position to be seen and admired by boys from all over the west side of Cincinnati. This included those who were bigger and better looking than me—and taller than her. And it seemed that nearly all of them could fast dance.

I was ready to twirl around and go home, acknowledge defeat before it was handed to me. But then Mary Ann and her friend

Maureen stepped into the hall. I was going nowhere. The thought of Mary Ann's bare arms around my neck while my hands rested on her waist and maybe her butt—now covered in denim—made my spirits do a 180.

I both fast and slow danced that night, afraid to leave Mary Ann alone in a crowd of competitors. During one slow dance, Mary Ann pulled me closer. I didn't resist. We were now cheek to cheek again. Her soft, moist skin felt better than any previous touch. Her perfume and her sweet breath on my neck were too much. I became aroused and recalled the stages of excitement that we learned about in sex-ed. But I didn't bother fighting it this time. I would let tonight unfold as it would. There would be plenty of time to say extra prayers and perform extra good deeds tomorrow.

"I really like you, Mary Ann," I said, shocking myself that I actually found the courage to say it.

"I really like you, too," she said. Her voice softer than her skin.

Neither of us knew what else to say. Maybe there wasn't anything else to say. With each sway, I thanked God and counted my blessings, secure once again in Mary Ann's presence—and in the presence of the church whose bells I thought I heard strike 10 o-clock.

After the slow dance, I fetched some drinks for me and my girl. When I returned, I found Mary Ann leaning against a stone wall. Behind her was an indoor grotto honoring the Virgin. Where else would my Mary Ann be? It felt so good to see her there, but also so wrong. I didn't need *anybody's* mother reminding me to be good. Not now. I avoided eye contact with the statue.

"Do you have the itch to crown *every* Mary you see?" I said, pointing behind us toward the Virgin.

"I'm just so glad all that crowning business is over."

"You looked really good doing it."

"I felt stupid."

"You're *not* stupid," I said, shocked at the mere suggestion. "What are you taking at Seton this year?" Elizabeth Ann Seton was the all-girls Catholic school right next door to Elder.

"Just the usual stuff, English, math, and all that. How about you?"

"The same, plus German."

"I'm taking Spanish."

"I'm sure you'll get straight A's, señorita," I said. Mary Ann laughed. I melted. I stood before her. She was still leaning against the rock wall, so we were eye to eye. She then asked what I wanted to do, and I responded with the very debonair, "I don't know, what do *you* want to do?"

The next thing I knew, we were making out. The lump in my pants was now a bulge, if not a downright protuberance. But I didn't care. Her lips were so soft I half expected them to melt away. The din of the other 150 kids talking, screaming, and singing had mellowed to a faint murmur. My own heart beat louder. If I could have been hooked up to a machine to feed me and take care of my bodily functions, I would have gladly stood there kissing Mary Ann forever. And ever.

Overcome with my good luck—and perhaps for the first time thinking with my hormones rather than my head—I ran my hands up and down Mary Ann's back, occasionally even working up the nerve to touch the top of her butt. I made a mental note to say some extra prayers that night. Was it okay to thank God for girl's butts? "God created *everything*," Sister Lucy said. I assumed, therefore, that the answer was a definite "yes."

We made out for an hour until the dance was nearly over. J.C. and Mary Ann's friend Maureen stopped by every fifteen minutes or so to check on us. Maureen called me "lover boy." J.C. whispered "stud" into my ear.

During one of the breaks when we came up for air, we talked about choosing our song. We settled on McCartney's "'Listen to What the Man Said." It really didn't matter what song was chosen, I thought. It just had to be one of McCartney's.

We went back to the dance floor for the final set and then kissed each other goodbye. Mary Ann was driven home by some friend's mother. J.C. and I walked home. He was going on and on about some girl he met, but I wasn't listening. I just thought about how Mary Ann could never do any wrong.

Summertime. A girl. Making out. It was a fantasy come true. But is was soon to come to an end. With a bang.

Chapter 16

Bottoms Up

Twenty minutes later, J.C. and I were sitting on the couch, each of us stroking our half-empty bottles as if they were cats on our laps. The older guys ignored us, lost in their own conversation about the building superinten-dent, ticket scalping, and someone named Delilah *who dumped their friend Ronnie.* I could feel Ronnie's pain.

A cute girl named Kate and her family moved to Pleasure Drive near J.C.'s house. During the July 4th weekend, Kate had friends over while her parents were out for the evening. J.C. and I talked our way over. Within an hour, I was making out with one of Kate's friends, Kelly. She was a short brunette and a tad bit on the heavy side, but—her redeeming value—she was also a tad bit on the slutty side. Mary Ann was far from my mind. And Satan, who no doubt was proud of my indiscretion, was even further.

I learned two important lessons that night on Pleasure Drive. First, girls kiss differently. (Mary Ann kissed gently and didn't move her mouth much; Kelly created a suction around my mouth that would make a vacuum cleaner jealous.) Second, if you're going to make out on a well-lit front porch, you best not care about who may pass by.

One of the people I performed for unwittingly was Kim Berne, a good friend of Mary Ann's. The next day, July 4th, I got a call from Mary Ann, usually soft and cool as mud between your toes, now as hot as a Roman candle. She wanted to know if it was true. Had I kissed another girl? Lying to my mom was one thing, lying to the May Queen a different matter altogether. I had no choice but to confess.

Mary Ann dumped me like a spent piece of gum. All of a sudden, Pleasure Drive didn't seem so pleasurable.

That night my family left to view some holiday fireworks at a nearby drive-in; I stayed behind. I laid on my bed and listened to Boston sing "More Than a Feeling" over and over and over. I even shed a tear or two, especially when they sung about a "Mary Ann" walking away.

The protective wall I had worked hard to erect around me just took a major hit. My soul was exposed like the Star Trek *Enterprise* behind a disabled force field, Klingon battleships fast approaching.

The next day, J.C. and I rode the bus to the shopping center to buy some 45s at the record shop and some cherry Cokes at Woolworth's.

"Mary Ann found out about what I did the other night," I said, tapping my fingers against the seat in front of us.

"How?"

"Kim Berne saw me kissing Kelly."

"And she ratted on you?" J.C.'s eyes were wide.

"Yep."

"What did you tell Mary Ann?"

"I couldn't get a word out. She just dumped me."

J.C. was momentarily distracted as he about broke his neck looking out the window at a girl walking down the sidewalk wearing tight shorts and her bikini bathing suit top. He then turned back to me. "There's more fish in the ocean," he said, pointing backward to the good-looking catch-of-the-day.

"I suppose so."

"Besides, you can do better."

"Hmm." Now I looked intrigued.

"Don't get me wrong. Mary Ann is nice and all, but, well, she's nice and all."

"What do you mean?"

"There are girls who like to do more than just kiss on the lips."

J.C. then reminded me that there was another CYO dance that coming Friday back at St. Lawrence Church. But this time, he said, we were going to do it up right. Looking out for me as a good friend does, and wanting to help mend my broken heart, J.C. said he had a plan. It involved that reported cure for a broken heart: alcohol. He had befriended some guys in their late teens and early twenties who lived in a small apartment near St. Lawrence. They agreed to buy us some beer and to let us drink it at their pad before the dance.

Smarting from the pain of being dumped, worrying that the Devil would take advantage of my weakened condition without Mary Ann, I agreed to the plan, eagerly and happily. It would also, I figured, give me a glimpse of how Dad felt when he drank. It would be something of an experiment. I was still fond of science.

On the afternoon of the dance, the Fallen Angel swooped down and took control of my thoughts. I was sitting in the backyard reading Dad's *Runner's World* magazine. The bushes turned to cages with lizards, the garage doors became pencils, the picnic table a pinball machine, and the rusty garbage cans turned into machine guns. I would have sworn that my shirt was soaked in gasoline.

Too distracted to read anymore, and my stomach queasy, I thought beer that night would help. I had heard J.C.'s dad, the bartender, call it "medicine." I fell asleep for a few hours on the chaise lounge, my dreams as bizarre, perhaps more so, than the Devil's visit.

When I woke up, I took a shower and put on a new pair of corduroys along with a T-shirt I won at a five-mile road race. It had the Nike logo on it, and I thought that would help make me look athletic and handsome.

An hour before the dance, J.C. and I stepped into his friend's apartment, which sat above a dry cleaners. A couple of guys smoked at a dinette table, bits of dried paint and oatmeal stuck on one leg. Piles of dirty laundry sat on a threadbare love seat and in random spots around the main living area. A poster of Queen's Freddie Mercury clung, barely, on the back of the door. J.C.'s friend Dale offered us a cigarette. I was too attentive to my training to dare smoke anything. J.C. accepted. We were *both* ready to drink, though.

We each gave Dale five dollars. He walked to a convenience store across the street to buy our beer. He came back instead with a couple of bottles of wine. "You get more bang for the buck when you drink the grape," Dale explained in slurred speech that made it obvious he spoke from experience.

Twenty minutes later, J.C. and I were sitting on the couch, each of us stroking our half-empty bottles as if they were cats on our laps. The older guys ignored us, lost in their own conversation about the building superintendent, ticket scalping, and someone named Delilah who dumped their friend Ronnie.

I could feel Ronnie's pain.

"What kind of wine do you have?" J.C. asked me, reading the label on his own bottle.

"'Rosey Red,'" I answered. "How about you?"

"'Peppy Pink.'"

"This stuff tastes pretty good," I said, comparing it to the bitter wine at church.

"It's like punch."

"I could drink several bottles of this stuff. Are you feeling anything?"

"No. Not yet, anyway."

"Maybe it just takes a while."

We tapped our bottles together in a toast to maturity as we sat drinking fine wine in a sophisticated adult's apartment. A half-hour later, the bottles empty and our hosts now debating the meaning of the lyrics to America's "Ventura Highway," J.C. and I sat on the couch, all smiles.

"I'm still not feeling much, how about you?" I said.

"I'm perfectly fine. Watch." J.C. stood up and spun around on his heels. About ninety degrees short of a 360 he fell over, laughing, his head in a pile of dirty sweatsocks.

"You moron! You can't handle your alcohol. Let me show you how it's done."

I attempted the same maneuver but only made it halfway around before tumbling back on the couch, matching J.C. laugh for laugh.

"What are you going to do if you see Mary Ann tonight?" J.C. asked. "You going to tell her off?"

"Maybe," I said, knowing what I really wanted to tell her was that I was sorry.

Our high hosts complimented us on our amazing drinking abilities. But it came as no surprise to us. After all, drinking was in our blood. J.C.'s dad was a part-time bartender and mine was an accomplished drinker in his own right.

But I was way too happy for my buzz to be anything like Dad's. Since he only drank beer, I figured that it must be a downer, wine an upper. So I decided that I would only drink wine, a more sophisticated buzz. I'd leave the beer for Dad and others who didn't want to feel happy.

J.C. and I strolled to St. Lawrence, laughing hysterically at pigeons, litter, and even our own images reflected in storefront windows. Once inside St. Lawrence's bingo hall, we slid right onto the dance floor. I had a rhythm, an easiness about me that I didn't when I was on the very same floor but a month ago.

At the first break, I saw Mary Ann's friend Maureen and approached her. "Hey Maureen! How's it going? What have you been up to? Is Mary Ann here? Is she? Is she?"

Maureen grabbed my chin and turned my head twenty degrees to the left. Standing right next to her and looking better than ever was Mary Ann, the first love of my life. And the first woman to dump me. Maureen squeezed my face, pushing my lips together like a fish. Mary Ann shook her head in disgust and walked away.

"He can do better than you," J.C. shouted at her back, his left middle figure up high. I knocked his arm down. She may not have been my girlfriend any longer, but I still liked her. Always would, I thought. Besides, the holy office of the May Queen deserved respect.

J.C. pushed me toward the dance floor, where I fast danced with an ease I had not known before. I burned up the dance floor until the band's first break, during which I saw Mary Ann and Maureen talking to some older boys.

My stomach began to churn.

When the band started up again, I found the noise level nearly painful. I told J.C. that I was leaving. He pleaded with me to stay, but I held my ground and walked away. Outside, my head seemed to pound louder. I walked home, stopping a couple of times to barf into some strangers' shrubs.

I was sure proud of myself. The drink filled me with confidence and something entirely new: rhythm. The drinking was worth the puking.

As I neared home, I couldn't shake thoughts of Mary Ann. She was no doubt fast dancing with an older guy, maybe even slow dancing. It was only a matter of time, I supposed. I did, however, have to replace her with someone, something, *anything* to help keep the Devil at bay.

Fortunately, an opportunity presented itself. Working for the church would be my salvation.

Chapter 17

A Ladder to Rome

In short, the project meant that my fellow volunteers and I had to stamp-by-hand more than a hundred thousand tickets. Our payment would come in the form of carbonated sugar water. Slaves in China were better compensated. But this, at least for me, was a labor for the Lord. My payment was not of this world.

J.C. and I attended a St. William youth club "open house" largely to see what kinds of girls could be found there. While we stuffed our faces with pretzels and potato chips, Becky Kent, a pimply sophomore, pitched us on membership. "The club sponsors dances every couple of weeks, a couple of camp-outs each summer, and lots of parties," she said. That was enough to make instant recruits out of us. The prospect of camping with girls, pimples or not, captured not only my full attention but my entire imagination.

Most of my classmates had no interest in the youth group. Anything affiliated with the church was generally seen as uncool. Not by me, of course. Becoming a card-carrying member of the Catholic Youth Organization would make me one of the Pope's official soldiers. That would be the equivalent of a hundred or more religious points. What choice did I have but to join?

One of the club's upperclassmen was Rick Demming, a gregarious, smart, and funny guy who had a cross tattooed on his right forearm. He described the group's mission and purpose, and outlined its structure. We learned the duties and responsibilities of the president, vice president, secretary, treasurer, and sergeant-at-arms. Such order was impressive. It was also in keeping with the hierarchy the church promoted, with which we were all rather comfortable. Youth group leaders were the first in a long line of decision-makers reaching all the way up to the head honcho himself: Pope Paul VI.

In addition to the executive roles, Rick informed everyone that keeping the group running smoothly required committed volunteers to fill other positions. These, he made a point of emphasizing, provided excellent training ground for future executive board members. And, as a matter of fact, one such underling position—publicity chairperson—was currently available to any interested, qualified person, including us newcomers.

To hold a leadership position in the youth group would no doubt strengthen the demon-fighting powers of membership. I raised my hand, prepared to battle anyone for the position and to take whatever oath of office the position required. It turned out to be a moot point, for no one else was interested. And there was no oath to recite. I did, however, take immediate ownership of the implements of office: tape, posterboard, and a plastic bag of largely dried-up markers.

It was my duty to prepare posters promoting the group's various fund-raisers: dances, car washes, and bake sales. And, Rick informed me, I had work to do: the group was sponsoring a doughnut breakfast after the 9:00 A.M. Mass in two weeks. Posters had to be up in the back of church in less than a week. It was my first assignment, my first chance to shine as a papal publicist.

Over the next two days, I handcrafted a baker's dozen of the posters. I labored over each one, ensuring that all the pertinent details were spelled out: date, place, and time. And I decorated each with crude but colorful illustrations of a doughnut, a glass of orange juice, and a cup of coffee.

A couple days later, during the club's volleyball team practice, I proudly showed my posters to Rick. He chastised me. He pointed to the word "doughnut" on the posters and said, referring to a better-off eastside parish, "You're using St. Vivian spelling. Around here we spell them d-o-n-u-t-s." Ashamed, I offered to redo them, but Rick said the posters had to get up right away. Besides, he said, they would still work, just not as well.

My first official act of leadership was a disappointing one. I worried that no one would show up for the doughnut breakfast, a parishwide protest against my highbrow spelling. To my relief, however, the attendance was solid, and our group made nearly eighty-five dollars. Though flawed, my posters worked. More importantly, I retained my position as chief publicist, banging out dozens of posters for other fund-raisers, editing out any big words.

The fund-raisers help cover the cost of attending the annual archdiocesan youth convention. Some five hundred high school kids gathered at a summer camp for a long weekend of workshops, prayer, and general horsing around. In exchange for the hard work I had accomplished with markers and posterboard, I was invited to attend the preconference sessions, which started a day earlier and were devoted to leadership development.

I had been given the nod. "We see a lot of potential in you," Rick told me as he shared the news. "We expect that you may be president of the youth club someday." I nodded humbly while imagining myself at some elaborate inaugural ceremony. Holding such a position would mean perhaps a thousand good points, maybe more.

One of the more attractive aspects of the youth convention was that it would keep me away from home for three nights. Such absences, which would become increasingly frequent, created some guilt. My mom and siblings would have to fend for themselves if Dad got a bit testy after tossing back a few beers. I wouldn't be around to help keep Dad in a good mood or, failing that, to absorb my fair share of the venom. Dad was never one to throw plates or punches. His weapons were words, words that stung even when you knew they weren't true, even when they were aimed at someone else. But for me the intoxicating freedom of being away and accruing spiritual benefits overpowered the guilt. Besides, many a saint and prophet had to abandon friends and family in order to serve the Lord.

That summer's youth convention sealed my involvement in the church. The five hundred kids that descended upon the camp gave me a sense of a religious community beyond my own parish. Here were a bunch of young people anxious to have fun, yet quick to praise the Lord, too. In some circles, such willingness to openly talk about Jesus would have gotten me laughed at. But not here. We went to Mass—uncoerced—every day. I could even cross and double-cross myself in public and it wouldn't raise a single suspicion among this group of Jesus Freaks.

I had found a new home, a place where the insincere and immature aspects of my faith, as well as the sincere and mature ones, slight though they were, could feel at ease.

At the convention banquet Saturday night, St. William was named "Youth Club of the Year." My friends and I knew our parish was special. It's the chief reason we called Price Hill "God's Holy Mountain," St. William's steeple its summit. And now our parish was publicly recognized as better than the others. Our youth group cheered and sung along with the band at the post-banquet dance. Between songs we shouted our cheer: "Uumph, en-gow-uh, St. William's got the pow-uh."

I joined in on the fun, too, but left early to walk outside under the country sky. I could barely believe all the stars—and my good luck. My youth group was considered the best in the entire archdiocese. And I was pegged as heir apparent to the throne. I knew that the Devil was going to have to try harder to get me now. And he did.

That very night, after climbing up the ladder to my top bunk inside a rustic, creaky cabin, I reviewed the day's events with J.C. in the bed below. But Satan had the last word. Shouts in my head mixed with the din of a cricket rock concert. I felt like I was swimming in their mating call. It was one of the relatively few visits to happen at night. The country darkness added an extra-dose of spookiness to the visit, sort of like watching the *Twilight Zone* with the lights off. "There's no rest for the wicked," Sister Lucy would often say. I had trouble getting to sleep that night.

The point of this message, postmarked Hell, was clear: Satan was willing to chase me up the ladder. And so up the rungs I climbed. As fast as I could. Posterboard and markers in hand.

My publicity efforts did not go unnoticed that summer. "We've got a special project that Father Kennedy and the youth group board have asked me to ask you about," my leader Rick said over the phone. "Given your good work with printed stuff, we knew this would be right up your alley."

Wow, I thought to myself, a brand new member and I'm already being called up for special duty. How could I say "no" to my youth group? My pastor? My Pope? How could I not keep stepping up the ladder, each rung closer to heaven? I agreed to do as needed without even knowing what that was.

"Great. Thanks for helping," Rick said. "Here's what we need: The summer festival is fast approaching and we have to label all of the raffle tickets."

A dozen or more booths at the festival sold raffle chances by the hundreds each hour over the three-day event. To help festival-goers keep track of what tickets came from what booth, the festival committee decided to label the back of each with a rubber-stamped descriptor: "Ham Booth," "Split the Pot," "$25 for 25¢."

In short, the project meant that my fellow volunteers and I had to stamp—by hand—more than a hundred thousand tickets. Our payment would come in the form of carbonated sugar water. Slaves in China were better compensated. But this, at least for me, was a labor for the Lord. My payment was not of this world.

Rick and I found about a half-dozen other recruits willing to join me in a non-air-conditioned school room, stamping our way to carpal tunnel syndrome. We made the most of it, though, listening to 8-tracks of the Bee Gees, Jackson Browne, and ELO while our mouths moved as fast as our hands.

"Did you know that Kenny liked Libby?" Missy Bokenkotter, a heavyset girl with owlish glasses, asked me and the other four stampers.

"You've got to be kidding me!" said Missy's skinny friend Ria Dickson. "She's a phony."

"Besides, I heard she has the hots for Tony Long," I said.

"Tony Long! That guy's a jerk," J.C. chimed in.

"Those two belong together," Allison Reid said. "The phony *and* the jerk."

"Speaking of jerks, what about Father Bunson?" Valerie said. "I heard he chewed out Nick Greene for not having his shoes shined."

"Who's going to the dance this weekend at St. Teresa?" I asked, wanting to change the subject. Priest bashing wouldn't do my soul any good.

"I'll go if you promise to dance with me," Ria said, winking at me.

"Sure, I'll dance with you," I said. Ria wasn't the prettiest girl in town, but she wasn't the ugliest either. Besides, a guy like me couldn't be too picky. In addition, I would one day need her vote when I ran for the youth group presidency.

We had to talk loud in order to be heard over the music and the pounding of our stamping. Each of us found his or her own technique and rhythm. For me, it was ink the rubber stamp once, and then apply it to three chances.

Thud. Whack—whack—whack.

God. Father—Son—Spirit.

Please. Kill—the—Devil.

Chapter 18

Popularity Bank

Who was I to complain about hallucinations and mind-splitting headaches when Jesus suffered death? So I offered up all of my pain to the glory of Jesus. I even gave myself a taste of crucifixion in his honor.

Within weeks, if not days, of entering high school, you are sized up and labeled. And the label, whether accurate or not, can be hard to peel off. Fortunately, my running prowess helped me secure a solid position in the freshman class hierarchy at Elder. That's something that otherwise would have been impossible for a skinny sissy like me in a class of 375 boys.

Running didn't bring the rank and privilege of playing football or basketball, but cross-country was nonetheless highly regarded at Elder. Preceding my arrival, the school sent a team to the state AAA cross-country finals for twelve straight years.

So long had I been anticipating running for Elder's "Purple Pack" that when I was given my uniform—purple nylon running shorts and a white, sleeveless jersey—I rushed home to try it on. I stood in my bedroom wearing my first official running uniform, imagining many a finish line tape breaking across my chest. Gone were the days when I had to do without uniforms or fashion my own. I had found my way to a place that respected the one thing that I could do better than most everyone. I was so overcome with joy that I cried, John Denver's "Sunshine on My Shoulders" playing on the radio.

Elder sat right next door to Elizabeth Ann Seton High School, home to a thousand girls in white blouses and plaid skirts. Every morning, dozens of Elder guys and their Seton gals congregated in the alley that divided the two campuses. Frisky couples held hands, tickled one another, and sometimes even made out. On the fringes of the crowd off of school property, the burn-outs puffed on cigarettes while their car stereos blared Led Zeppelin, The Who, and the Rolling Stones.

As a freshman, I mostly viewed this carnal pleasure from inside the building. Though intriguing, it was, after all, an inappropriate place for a youth leader, a Roman soldier, a flag waver for Jesus. Besides, I usually attended a brief eucharistic service in the chapel with a dozen students and a few faculty members. Though sucking face with a girl would have been my preferred way to kick off the day, the high school life presented new temptations and distractions for which I needed my Daily Bread. And it never hurt to squeeze in a request for mental clarity on those days when an algebra test would be laid down on my desk.

I praised God in other ways, too. A poster hanging at Elder read: "Jesus gives us nothing we can't handle." It depicted a tiny boat, its mast broken in half, about to be swallowed whole by an enraged sea. I saw myself as that battered vessel. If this poster spoke the truth, and I believed that it did, then I was chosen, special, even blessed. Only a young man of considerable strength, endurance, and faith would be given such a burden as mine to shoulder. Besides, who was I to complain about hallucinations and mind-splitting headaches when Jesus suffered death? So I offered up all of my pain to the glory of Jesus. I even gave myself a taste of crucifixion in his honor.

When you run forty to seventy miles a week, you wear through shoes, especially the heels, quickly. My fellow runners and I often used hot glue to build up our worn soles. But once I decided to try those hard plastic heel taps intended for dress shoes. I attached a pair to my blue-and-gold Nike Waffle Trainers, confident the heel taps would last longer than the hot glue.

Running a few miles before school one morning, I felt a sharp pain in my right heel. It disappeared quickly, but then came back a few minutes later. It disappeared again, but then reappeared within seconds and remained. I thought a sharp pebble had worked its way into my shoe. I stopped, sat on the curb, and pulled off my right shoe and sock. My heel was bloody.

I licked a couple of fingers and then wiped the blood away exposing a tiny hole in my foot. I turned my shoe upside down and knocked it against the curb, expecting to dislodge a rock. Nothing came out. I put my hand in the shoe and felt around. I pulled back the sole liner, exposing the source of my pain: One of the brad nails that I foolishly used to attach the heel tap had worked its way up through my shoe, poking me in the foot with every stride.

As I prepared to yank the nail out, a thought came quickly to me. Why not leave it there and finish my run, offering the pain up to Jesus, a small taste of his agony on the cross? I was only about a mile from school where I would take a shower and change before my first class. I half-ran and half-hobbled the rest of the way, passing any number of kids walking to school. Several of them, unaccustomed to seeing me run while limping and grimacing, asked if I was okay. "Cramp," I responded through my clenched teeth. I hobbled on, losing blood while praising Jesus for his. Is it any wonder, therefore, that God blessed me with a fair amount of success on the cross-country course that fall?

One thing that I especially liked about cross-country was that, while technically a team sport, I didn't have to rely on teammates the way that, say, a baseball or football player must. I could walk away with a win, place, or show, as I typically did, regardless of how the rest of the team performed. Since there was so much at stake for me, I couldn't imagine having to rely on a teammate to toss me a ball or throw a block. As it turned out, the freshman team at Elder was solid, scoring well in all its meets. This made me doubly happy. Jesus, too.

I ran every weekday with the team, usually three to ten miles. Once or twice a week, Head Coach Glenmary and Assistant Coach Ehrlich would toss in some speed work. On those days, we freshmen would run a couple of miles to warm up, then as many as ten quarter-mile sprints, followed by a two-mile warm down. Sometimes the coaches prescribed *fartlek*, a long, slow jog interspersed with sprints, some up to a quarter-mile long.

Our meets usually fell on Saturday mornings. We raced two miles through a park or golf course, or over a school's grounds. I preferred hilly courses through woods. The hillier the terrain, the better I performed. And wooded courses were simply prettier, especially later in the fall. The bright red and orange leaves against a crisp blue October sky helped keep my mind off the burning sensation in my legs and lungs.

No other Elder freshman beat me in a race that season. I was faster than many of the team's sophomores, juniors, and even some of the seniors. At the Elder Invitational, I ran the hilly two-mile course at Rapid Run Park in 10:52. Only one other freshman in the school's history had run it faster, and just by two seconds. I also won the freshman division in the Greater Catholic League championships, the meet that brought together teams from six large Catholic high schools in Cincinnati.

Fortunately for me, the results of the cross-country meets were announced every Monday morning at school. Each time my name was spoken over the PA, I earned a deposit in the popularity bank. It was security, too. No one would dare mess around with one of the Purple Pack's best. That would be toying with history and tradition. The Catholic Church had taught us to honor both.

At the end of my freshman cross-country season, I joined some juniors and seniors (who were not running in the state championship meet) for a full marathon sponsored by the Ohio River Roadrunners Club. We ran on the same country road that Dad had competed on through the years. The course went out and back—twice. We marathoners had nothing to look at for 26.2 miles but mostly empty cornfields. I was the first Elder runner to cross the finish line. My time, three hours and fifteen minutes. I was hoping to break three hours.

Dad drove me and three other exhausted members of the Purple Pack home in the Beige Bomber. We had to stop once for Gary St. Claire to puke up what seemed like several gallons of lime-green Gatorade.

As Dad drove south on I-75 it occurred to me that I had turned into a better runner than he was—or would likely ever be. I glanced at him, his eyes on the road, his mouth going nonstop about the marathon. Frank Shorter, this, Bill Rodgers that.

Part of me took great delight in the realization that I could kick my old man's rear in anything longer than a sprint. Some of it was the natural urge any son has to one-up his father. Some of it was likely the sweet taste of revenge. Dad may have the upper hand at home, especially when drinking, but he wouldn't on the

The midway point of the Monroe Marathon.

open road. That was my turf. And he couldn't do or say anything to stop me. Of course part of me was saddened by my realization. But that day—whether I wanted to or not—I took a giant step away from Dad, a step that all sons must at some point or another. My step measured twenty-six miles and change.

My performance in the marathon was announced over the PA on Monday morning. I received countless high fives from fellow students throughout the day as I walked stiff-legged from class to class.

The Devil paid me a visit that day, too, as he was apt to do at Elder. He approached me in the cafeteria. I just sat for a moment with my head bent like I was saying grace. The rest of the afternoon shot, I doodled rather than take notes in class.

I did all I could to appear ordinary. If I was to be seen as extraordinary in any way, I wanted it to be for my running. Or my involvement in school and church activities. Or my way with the ladies. The least little weakness spotted in someone was reason for teasing or some harassing. No one would suspect me. I wouldn't give them a reason to.

I had every reason to keep running my butt off and pray like a man possessed. Something weird, very weird, was in the works, for 1978 was the year of three popes. Pope Paul VI died on August 6. He was succeeded by John Paul I on August 26. That pope died but thirty-four days later. On October 16, he was succeeded by John Paul II.

This was further evidence that everything happens in threes, as Grandma Marge said. But three popes in one year? No one could have imagined it. Popes were supposed to live—and rule—for a long time. This was a sign. I knew it. Grandma Marge knew it. She just wasn't sure of what. I thought I had a clue.

Chapter 19

Wet Kisses

> I kept slapping the gavel into my hand,
> unaware of the welt emerging in my palm. As
> for doing God's work, it seemed as if I was
> damned if I did, and damned if I didn't. But
> my instincts told me to keep doing. The beer
> helped, too.

Bishop—Cardinal—Pope. Nerd—Pothead—Quarterback. Clearly, rank mattered. And though I certainly rose in stature when I accepted the responsibilities of youth group publicity chair, leading a committee of one wasn't very impressive in anyone's eyes, let alone God's. So after a year of scribbling posters and mimeographing fliers, I decided to run for youth club president. Now that was a position that would mean something—to me and to Jesus.

Over a Big Mac lunch one Sunday afternoon, I sought counsel from my trusted advisor on all things important: J.C.

"I'm thinking about running for president," I said.

"Of the United States?" J.C. asked, special sauce on his lip.

"No, dork, of the youth club."

"Take it easy, spaz, I was just kidding. You should do it."

"Do you think I'll win?" I really wasn't the least bit concerned with whether or not I was qualified to hold the office. All that mattered were my odds. I couldn't risk running and losing.

"Connie Gest may run," J.C. said.

"She's a bit too quiet, don't you think?"

"She's nice. But not as nice as *that*," J.C. said, nodding toward two girls sitting at the back of the restaurant.

"They're foxes," I said. "But what about Connie?"

"She's a nice girl."

"You said it."

"Said what?" J.C. asked.

"*Girl.*"

"So?"

"So that's my point." I said, waving a french fry at him.

"What point?"

"That Connie's a *girl*. Guys are better leaders," I said. By virtue of the fact that I had a penis, I was, theoretically speaking, in a position to rise all the way to the top, to sit on a throne and make infallible, papal proclamations. Why put a girl in a position with no real, long-term future? It made sense to me then, though years later I would cringe at such a sexist thought.

"Boys may be better leaders, but girls are better looking," J.C. said.

"So you think I should run?"

"Sure, why not?" J.C. said. He then began speaking in a high-pitched voice, shifting his head left and right, resting his elbows on the table, letting his hands both go limp at the wrist. "Oh, Mr. President, how can I *serve* you? How about I chair the *social* committee and the two of us have the first committee meeting right here, *together.*"

"Stop it," I said, flicking a fry at him. J.C.'s little act embarrassed me some, but I believed his point to be true: Girls dig men in power. That alone was reason to run.

As it turned out, I ran unopposed for youth group president. I wanted to believe that's because others considered me either unbeatable or absolutely perfect for the job. Truth was, no one wanted the hassles. Or, more to the point, no one *needed* the hassles the way I did.

Though unopposed, I still felt it necessary to prepare and deliver a campaign speech. I had not forgotten lessons learned from the eighth-grade talent show: 1) presentation matters, and 2) everything is better with a little theater.

In St. William's undercroft, I stood wearing a tie before twenty members, most of whom were talking among themselves. I cleared my throat and delivered my speech:

For the past year, St. William's youth group has played a major part of my life. Since I became a member, I have taken an active role in many activities, far too numerous to name them all now. Besides attending many youth club events like dances, picnics, parties, and summer convention, I have offered my ideas, opinions, and suggestions at regular, board, and special projects meetings.

I am very familiar with how youth club operates and what is to be expected from each board member. There is no doubt in my mind—and there should be no doubt in yours—that I have more than enough experience to be president.

I believe we need a more unified board with better communication within it. Summer is right around the corner and I want to see campouts, canoe trips, picnics, Reds games, and horseback riding on the agenda.

I want St. William's youth club to become more involved with youth groups on the eastern side of the city to destroy the wall between us.

I'm experienced, willing, and capable.

I'm Steve Kissing.

I'm your man *for president.*

I won everyone's vote, discounting the two that were cast for write-in candidates Peter Frampton and Mork of TV's *Mork and Mindy*. At least these jokesters had the sense to vote for a man, I thought at the time.

Outgoing president Stew Kylie presented me with the symbol of my new office and authority: a wooden gavel. After the election and hanging out with my new followers in the undercroft, I walked home. Proud. Confident.

Whistling while twirling the gavel in my fingers, I thought about how the gavel was another totem to my goodness, to my devotion to the church and her husband: Jesus Christ. I began to tap the gavel in my palm. I slowly increased the force with each swing, each one a symbolic whack upside the head of the Evil Wizard. It occurred to me that my new position brought with it considerable pressure.

I wasn't worried so much about the responsibilities of my new role, but rather what would happen if I was discovered. It would be one thing for a troublemaker or a burn-out to be recognized as the Devil's plaything. But it would be something else altogether if the president of St. William's youth group were so fingered. Imagine that! Such scandal would rock St. William and maybe all of CYO to its core.

It occurred to me then that maybe I wasn't doing God's work after all. Maybe I was just being outsmarted by Satan, pushed higher and higher until he deemed the time ripe to expose me. Or force me to perpetrate acts against the church from deep inside.

I kept slapping the gavel into my hand, unaware of the welt emerging in my palm. As for doing God's work, it seemed as if I was damned if I did, and damned if I didn't. But my instincts told me to keep doing.

J.C. and me

The beer helped, too.

Every Sunday, St. William parishioners had the option of attending two Masses at 11:00 a.m.: Traditional Mass upstairs in the church, with organ, choir, and four altar boys, or the Guitar Mass downstairs in the undercroft with folding chairs, makeshift altar, and two altar boys. J.C. had taken to playing the guitar and joined a few other strummers up front leading us in song. I envied his musical ability. Chicks dug guys who played the guitar. J.C. got his fair share. And then some.

J.C. and I earned five dollars every Saturday night by setting up chairs in the undercroft for the Guitar Mass. After erecting the altar and putting two hundred chairs in place, we would walk into the large kitchen area for our refreshments. We would take a five-gallon, stainless-steel coffee urn from a cabinet and position it under the draft beer tap the church had, unwatched, in the kitchen. We would fill the urn halfway, then walk out, each holding a handle. I would have preferred wine, but the beer was sure easier to come by. And it didn't seem to irritate me as it did Dad.

We'd then carry our brew as delicately as possible—so as to not create unwanted foam. We perched ourselves across the street atop a short but steep hill behind J.C.'s house. One night, after a buzz settled in, we complimented each other.

156

"I toast you and the Purple Pack, the finest bunch of runners ever," J.C.said, raising his paper cup, beer spilling out the side.

"And I toast your guitar playing," I said, wiping foam off my lip. "You're the next James Taylor."

"I toast Amy Witt," he said, "the best-looking girl in Price Hill."

"And I double-toast Suzie Ryker," I said. "The sexiest girl in the entire world."

"And I toast Price Hill, God's Holy Mountain."

"I toast St. William, his favorite church," I said.

"Next to St. Peter's Basilica, of course," J.C. corrected me.

"Of course."

Using the keys we were given to get inside the undercroft, we'd return the urn. We'd then walk around the neighborhood, sometimes rolling down grassy lawns to see if either of us would puke. We'd lie at the bottom of people's front yards and stare at the sky, spitting up and laughing, until a porch light turned on and chased us away.

On some warm nights we'd go streaking. We'd hide behind a bush at St. William, take off our clothes, and wait for the traffic light at the intersection to turn red. We'd then dash across the busy street in front of unsuspecting motorists, our underwear on our heads, the warm air embracing our bodies, our sweat glistening in the glow of headlights.

One night after setting up for Guitar Mass, J.C. and I had gotten wind that a couple of girls from youth group were babysitting at a nearby house. Emboldened by the liquid courage we stole from the church, we knocked on the door after midnight. The girls, most of them a year or two older, were all smiles and giggles. I noticed empty beer and wine bottles on the kitchen table.

Within minutes, J.C. and I were giving and receiving kisses from the girls, our heads spinning from the booze—and our hormone surge. Not long after, I found myself in a bedroom with Kim

157

Berne, the same girl who ratted me out to Mary Ann last July 4th weekend. I fell back on the bed. Kim shut the door and laid on top of me. It was my first time with a girl in a dark bedroom. And an older girl at that. We began to kiss. Kim slid her tongue in my mouth. This was new to me. Odd but wonderful. I didn't know what to do, so I just did what seemed to make the most sense: I shoved my tongue into her mouth. I tasted wine and cigarette smoke.

Way too soon, Kim and I heard a bang on the door. Lisa Bazler said she wanted a turn. That was okay by me. Lisa was better looking and she didn't smoke. Kim just smiled, stood up, and walked out, blowing me a kiss, asking where J.C. was. Lisa shut the door and laid right next to me, stroking my hair, and sucking on my neck. We then began to kiss. I thrust my tongue in her mouth. She snaked her tongue into mine.

Within minutes, Carey Lancefort walked in and told us to break it up. Her sister and brother-in-law were due home any minute. She said the place looked and smelled like a Texas whorehouse and if we didn't clean it up, we were all going to be facing the wrong end of her brother-in-law's six-shooter. Carey asked J.C. and me to take some grocery bags full of empty bottles with us and ditch them in the woods. Each with a bag in hand, and our clothes slightly askew, J.C. and I hightailed it out of the house.

Outside, we put our arms around each other and walked down the street, propping each other up. Less than a block away, we tossed the bags of empty bottles behind a parked car.

It was the best night of our lives. Multiple kisses from multiple girls. Tongue included. There was a God. No doubt about it.

"I wish every night was like this night," J.C. said.

"That would be heaven," I said, twirling my tongue in circles, trying to get its normal feeling back.

I was elated, but feeling nauseous. I bid J.C. a good night.

As I walked home alone, however, I panicked. I began to wonder what kind of germs or sexually transmitted diseases I may have picked up having had two wet tongues in my mouth. These were tongues of older women, one even a senior. No telling where those tongues had poked and prodded before. I recalled those horrible images of open sores from sex-ed class. My tongue felt full and tingly. Early warning signs, I thought.

Once home, I boiled some water and made tea. Taking a cue from Grandpa Elmer, I even put a dab of bleach in the water for extra measure. For five minutes, I took sips and gargled with the steamy liquid. My tongue stung a little, but I was convinced it would help prevent the spread of disease. And it was fair torture for such naughty behavior.

My penance would be more church work. I seized every opportunity to score ever more points with Jesus.

Though I was no longer serving Mass, I had, with the encouragement of Father Rob, a hip parish priest who played the electric guitar, become a lay distributor, placing the Holy Host in the hands of those seeking God's meal. I didn't fully appreciate at the time just what a big deal this was. For just a relative few years earlier, only priests were empowered to dispense Communion. Now even a possessed kid could do the honors.

Just as I brought reverence and theater to serving, so I did with distributing Communion. I was always certain to hold the host up in front of the recipients' eyes when I said, "The Body of Christ." I then slowly and deliberately placed the host in their hands or, if they preferred the old-fashioned way, on their tongues.

I asked Father Rob if I could give the homily after the Gospel reading some Sunday. He said yes, even though this was a real no-no. While occasionally a visiting priest or nun could use the homily to talk about missionary work or the religious life, the homily was not intended to be delivered by a layperson, particularly one just fifteen years old.

This was my biggest opportunity at Devil-busting yet. For two weeks, I wrote and rewrote my remarks and practiced them in front of the bathroom mirror. I put on my best threads for the homily: a light-brown vest and sport coat, dark brown pants, and a tie with every imaginable hue of brown. I thought I looked better than ever.

Delivering my first—and only—homily in the undercroft of St. William's Church.

This confidence helped me deliver the sermon with real punch, and one hand in my pocket:

As in every December, people are beginning to prepare for Christmas: buying gifts, putting up decorations, holding parties. Everyone's in good spirits, feeling well. There's a lot of love evident. Everyone's looking forward to the good times of Christmas. But why only once a year?!

For Christ, one Christmas is not enough. Jesus is not just a moment in past history. Jesus chose to be born again and again and again every day through each person. God urges us to take on the same mission as his apostles. God also urges us to be like John the Baptist and to continuously prepare the world for the birth of his son.

We are called to celebrate the birth of Christ every day of the year. We as Christians are to be his hands and his feet, to truly live the Gospels. It is our responsibility to seek out how Christ wants us to represent him in today's world.

The calling may be to raise a family, to be a fireman, carpenter, or lawyer. Or perhaps you are called to become active in parish activities to help with the senior citizens of St. William. Or to be an adult advisor for the youth club. And we are to fulfill our calling to the fullest by taking on the image of Christ, to be his hands and feet.

All Christians share one calling in common, that of becoming a living image of Christ. When Jesus was born into the world, he completely changed it.

As it was said in the Gospel, "Every valley shall be filled and every mountain be leveled." As Christ changed the world with a group of ignorant fisherman, so, too, can we if we take on his image and become one with him through the Eucharist. If only we truly let the light of the world shine on us—every day of the year.

After Mass, many parishioners, young and old, thanked me for my comments and patted me on the back. More than a few said that I could really preach. For the first time, I began to think that maybe I was being called to the priesthood.

Of course, my fellow parishioners only knew the public me: the winning athlete, the youth group president, the sermon maker. They didn't know the private me: the beer drinker, the womanizer, Satan's toy.

I was a wolf in sheep's clothing.

Chapter 20

An Altar-ed State

> Jesus had the Shroud of Turin, a sheet from his burial that was imprinted with a likeness of his crucified body; I had a holy water-stained pullover shirt that captured my imagined wounds.

St. William's Church was not only my protector, the seat of my youth leadership power, and the primary source of my beer, it was also my employer. In grade school, I made a few extra bucks selling *Cincinnati Enquirers* and shoveling snow around the church. For a while in high school, I spent a couple of nights each week working at the rectory, the priest's spartan, yet comfortable, residence connected to the back of the church.

Working in the rectory made me feel like a real insider. I occasionally overheard bits of conversation: a priest passionately trying to convince married couples to stay together; a parishioner complaining about pigeon poop. I saw priests in the kitchen with soup dripping off their chins. I saw them in the living room watching TV, laughing at the same jokes I did. I even saw Father Kennedy in street clothes. Just once. I literally did a double-take.

It took several seconds for me to recognize him when he came into view wearing brown shoes, tan pants, and a light brown golf shirt. It would be like seeing the Virgin Mary in jeans.

Most visitors came to meet with priests to make funeral arrangements for a loved one or for counseling of some sort. Others came to purchase miracles.

For a small donation, one could have a Mass dedicated to a loved one. This allegedly cured the sick, freed prisoners, and made the dumb smart. It also helped score points for tortured souls stuck in purgatory and in dire need of a little push upward. Run-of-the-mill weekday Masses cost three dollars. The more potent Sunday and Holy Day Masses went for five bucks. I assumed that God appreciated the extra cash.

I had not really known at the time that the church had a rich tradition of selling Masses and indulgences of all sorts. I simply took my fellow parishioners' money and wrote the name of their loved one in the Mass log. I then informed them which Mass was "theirs" and gave them an attractive greeting card as a memento. There were two cards to choose from. One was tan and somber and featured a crucifix. It was for those who bought a Mass for the dead. The other card, for the living, featured a sparkling rainbow.

This choice meant I had to ask the person purchasing the Mass whether it was for someone alive or dead. This was, of course, a hard question to pose. Most who came to buy Masses were elderly. Their loved one could have been lying in a hospital bed gasping for their last breath, or six feet under pushing up daisies. I developed a knack for reading their eyes, for discerning the difference between hope for the living and hope for the dead. Those seeking aid for the living would look you right in the eye; those trying to help the dead looked everywhere but at you, as if expecting to catch a glimpse of their loved one walking down the hallway.

If a Mass could help some poor soul on the verge of death or sweating it out in purgatory, it could certainly help me. So I ponied up the money. I felt a bit odd buying a Mass for myself; it felt self-indulgent. But it didn't stop me. I put five dollars, a third of my weekly salary, in the metal lockbox and pulled out a rainbow card. The inside read: "This Mass is being said in honor of _____. May this child of God live in happiness." I carefully printed my name on the blank line, inserted the card in the envelope, and then slid it gently into my bookbag.

A Sunday Mass six months hence would be said in my name. Almost immediately, I felt better. And smart. It would do wonders for my soul. I was sure of it.

Lucifer came to the rectory several times. He never asked for a Mass to help get his own sorry butt out of Hades. He just asked for me. The rectory, with religious paintings and artifacts everywhere you looked, was a creepy place to have an encounter with the Priest of Horrors.

The library-like quiet that permeated the rectory made the voices in my head seem louder. But, on the positive side, the lack of noise helped calm my post-visit nerves, as did the ice cream with chocolate sauce, always in plentiful supply in the rectory kitchen.

There were plenty of perks working in a rectory. For one, a priest was always available to hear my confession. In addition, I could use the phone and not worry about Mom overhearing my conversations.

"Hi Linda, it's Steve."

"Why are you whispering?"

"I'm calling from the rectory."

"What are you doing there?"

"Working."

"Working?"

I figured it never hurt to let girls knows that priests trusted me. That way, whenever I tried to get physical with them they would be less likely to protest. Perhaps they would even see it as an extension of my church work.

"Yeah, I answer the phone and things."

"That's cool."

"So you can help at the car wash this Saturday?" I asked.

"Will I get wet?"

"Maybe just a little." Truth was, I hoped she got drenched. Barefoot girls in wet shorts and shirts. And who says working for the Pope doesn't have its privileges?

"Okay, then. I'll come."

"Bring some friends."

One of the other perks of working in the rectory was that holy water was most abundant. There was a receptacle in virtually every hallway. I crossed myself so much with the blessed fluid that I permanently stained one of my favorite shirts on my belly, left and right shoulders. Jesus had the Shroud of Turin, a sheet from his burial that was imprinted with a likeness of his crucified body; I had a holy water–stained pullover shirt that captured my imagined wounds.

Another rectory perk was all the holy light.

With so little time at home, I mostly had to abandon my self-exorcisms. I replaced them with a light purification ceremony that I conducted at the rectory on weekend afternoons.

In some of the rectory hallways one could enjoy some small, beautiful stained-glass windows featuring deep blues, reds, and yellows. Sunlight would pour in, creating beams of soft color, tiny bits of dust floating inside them. When the coast was clear, I'd stand in the colored beams of light: red on my face, blue on my torso, yellow on my arms. I believed the light, having traveled through the images of religious icons, to be blessed, holy, potent.

I would stand still for five minutes or more, basking in this holy light, sure it was giving me strength. As the warm light soothed my face, I closed my eyes and said some prayers. I still said the standards, but I sometimes prayed freestyle:

Dear Jesus, you are the Light of the World. I ask you to fill me with your strength. May I follow your example and be open to your teachings. May I use my time and talent for good works. May I do everything I possibly can to stay out of the darkness.

One of my duties was locking up the church each night. I'd walk out on to the main altar, genuflecting while crossing myself, and then walk down the stairs toward the pews. Once on the main floor, I would lock the two side doors and the five in the rear. The only sounds were the crackling of the votive candles, the rustling of pigeons roosting outside on the ledges, and gusts of wind through the belfry.

I'd then walk back up on the main altar, feeling the stares of the Jesus, Mary, and Joseph statues on me as if some tangible beam of energy were coming from their marble eyeballs and warming my skin. On the altar, I would genuflect again, and then turn out the lights.

One night, shortly after a visit from Satan, when I made my way back to the main altar and genuflected, I stayed on my knee, bowed my head, and began to pray. I felt wobbly with my weight on my bony knee. So I lay face-down on the cool marble, resting my forehead on top of my hands. I took the same prostrate position as young men about to be ordained to the priesthood.

Fifty feet above me was a painting of Jesus sitting on top of a rainbow, the earth his footstool, a field of stars behind him. In his left hand was a book with the symbols of the alpha and the omega. His right hand was raised in a gesture of peace.

I prayed to God that he would use just a little of the power he relied on to create the heavens to rid me of my demons. I began

166

to cry a little. Within a few minutes I was sobbing, my tears dripping onto the marble altar, dusted every day. "Please—stop—this," I said, each word pushed out between gasps. "Please—please—please." My nose was running, globs of snot and drool falling onto the altar, pooling with my tears.

Then I snapped.

"I'm sick and tired of this bullshit—of this crazy, fucking bullshit!" I yelled. "I can't take it any more! I can't take any more of this crazy, fucking bullshit!" The screams echoed through the church and came back to me not as my voice but as someone else's. Someone in dire need of help. And very disrespectful. My own harsh words aimed at The Man Himself stunned me into silence. I couldn't believe I had talked to God that way, especially inside St. William, his second favorite church.

The Devil made me do it. I was still going to get it, even worse than when I talked back to Mom or Dad.

I stood up and wiped my face with my sleeve. I pulled my shirttails out of my pants and then knelt down and wiped the altar dry where I had defaced it. My eyes red, I walked back into the rectory, put the keys away, grabbed my bookbag, and walked home.

I hoped my prayers would be answered. But for the first time, I wondered, oh so briefly, if there was even a God to hear them. I dismissed this crazy idea and kept moving forward.

Chapter 21

Sinister Plan

And, besides, I couldn't tell them the best story I had. Claiming demonic possession before a group of young Jesus Freaks at a remote retreat center didn't seem real smart. I could darn near see the headlines: "Young Catholics Murder Devil's Agent."

The Devil kept coming. On a couple of occasions, several times a day. But to family, friends, and teachers—none of whom were around me all day, every day—my occasional zoning out wasn't enough to cause any concern. Helping me out was the fact that my friends and I would often act as if we were high, mimicking the burn-outs by talking as slowly as a permanent resident of a tropical island. Years after high school, a friend wrote me a note in which he said, *"In school you would occasionally space out in class or lunch but I never really caught on to that. I honestly thought you were screwing around. It wasn't until much later when you told me that you were having attacks—and that you worried that you were crazy or possessed—that I put it together."*

As the Devil turned on the heat, I devised a new plan: I would offer my suffering up to the Lord. I would turn a negative into a positive, a bad into a good, a pain into a pleasure. Satan thought he was bringing me down by inflicting pain. But since I was now dedicating my suffering to Jesus, I was growing closer to God, not drifting farther away. I turned the Devil's deeds into a heavenly hymn. I knew this would piss Satan off and, therefore, potentially intensify matters. But I was running out of options.

I was hopeful that my goodness was shining through for the world to see. I was encouraged when my younger brother, Dave, asked me to be his confirmation sponsor. I was, at least in his eyes, a model Christian. I, of course, agreed to sponsor him. The initial joy of his request was tarnished some when I learned that most of the kids in his class asked older brothers and sisters rather than aunts, uncles, and grandparents as was the trend in my day. I knew some of the other sponsors of Dave's class-mates well, for they were my age. Some were just dumb jocks, I thought, no-neckers who didn't care about Jesus the way I did.

In my quest for heavier doses of holy medicine, I attended youth retreats throughout the year. Each retreat was super-vised by a couple of adult mod-erators and a priest who stopped by to hear confessions and say Mass. But other young people largely ran the programs.

Dave and me prior to his confirmation.

Friday night was typically devoted to ice breakers, silly games that enabled the ten to twenty participants from different parishes to get to know one another. The "Adjective Game" was standard issue. Sitting in a circle, each person introduced him- or herself with an adjective that began with the same letter as his or her first name. I usually chose Slippery, Sly, or Stupendous Steve. But each time I toyed with introducing myself as "Satanic Steve." I never did. After going around the circle and meeting Punctual Patty, Rowdy Rick, Jolly Jody, and the others, one person chosen at random tried to introduce everyone by his or her adjective name.

After the introductions, one of the youth leaders would give witness to the power of the Lord in his or her life. We'd then say some prayers and read a bit of Scripture. Before going to bed, we'd devour snacks and pop, listen to music, and play board games.

Saturday was typically an emotional day for most. The retreat's adult and youth leaders gave testimony. Each would talk about the pain and suffering in his life and how the Lord helped him overcome it. Divorced parents. Delinquent siblings. Broken hearts. Occasionally, some would share more heavyweight topics: sibling suicide, parental depression, a widowed mother now playing the field like a hooker with a quota and a deadline. Tears were shed, hugs dispensed, prayers uttered.

Some of the participants would be so moved as to tell their stories, too. I, of course, had stories, but I wasn't about to tell them. Claiming demonic possession before a group of young Jesus Freaks at a remote retreat center didn't seem real smart. I could darn near see the headlines: "Young Catholics Murder Devil's Agent."

More to the point, there would be no hope of making out with a girl if I announced my affair with the Devil. So I kept my mouth shut about Satan, in hopes I would get the chance to open it near Merry Monica.

Saturday afternoon at the retreats was devoted to personal reflection. We were asked to write letters to Jesus or, if we so chose, to a parent or friend. We were to share our feelings with the recipient, perhaps clear up an issue, or thank him or her for caring.

As the participants wrote away, some were brought to tears. One of the retreat organizers would approach to provide comfort and counseling. To aid us in our reflection, music played softly from a portable record player. The retreat standards included albums from Bread, Styx, Chicago, John Denver, Jim Croce, Cat Stevens, and Seals & Crofts.

Music always helped my meditation. I and others believed that Jesus talked to us through popular songs.

In religion class at Elder, we were asked to write about our favorite tunes and the messages they delivered. Among the five I chose was "Fooling Yourself" by Styx. (Was it any wonder that a group named after the fiery river to hell would speak to me?)

For the class assignment, I wrote: *I really like this song by Styx because I feel it's one that Christ is singing to many depressed people. When I'm feeling down about something, this song can get me back on my feet and back out there fighting. The song also speaks of "sinister plans" which I interpret as evil that hides "a caring young man"—me.*

In a moment of weakness and indiscretion, I actually referred to my demons. The teacher didn't notice. I did, however, get an "A" on the paper.

After listening to music at the retreats on Saturday afternoon, I usually spent time alone outside. I'd go for a run through the woods. Stopping now and then to enjoy the view, I'd praise God and ask him to help Punctual Patty with her mean mom or Loony Lou with his butthead brother. Back at the retreat facility, I'd take a nap on my assigned bunk bed or try to strike up a conversation with a pretty girl.

Once when at retreat at an archdiocesan seminary, I entered the chapel with one of my favorite running trophies in hand. I thanked God for my running talent and then left the trophy sitting on the ledge of a stained-glass window where the faux gold and cheap chrome reflected the pastel light. God gave me the talent, so it seemed only fitting that he should have the hardware.

On retreat Saturday nights we'd eat dinner, typically spaghetti and meatballs. Then we'd go to confession and have Mass. Then it was time for snacks, hanging out, and more silly games.

Before bedtime, the group would gather to recite evening prayers. To create a stimulus and focal point for our praying, a technique called Zorch was often employed. This entailed hanging strips of plastic from the ceiling. The lights would be turned off. The plastic rope would be lit on fire, and bit by bit, a small piece would plummet to a pan on the floor like a shooting star dropping from the top of the sky toward the horizon.

I'd watch the little flames light up the room. I saw myself in those tiny bursts of light—all bright and shiny on the outside—but spiraling downward, fast, toward a bitter end.

The following morning, parents and friends and previous retreat "graduates" would arrive for a farewell Mass. The participants would stand holding hands near the altar, while friends and family sat on folding chairs. At the point when peace is shared via handshakes and hugs, tears usually flowed, a touching moment between family and friends. My parents came to a few of the retreat Masses, but I wasn't one to get all teary in front of them.

We'd then all go home. I'd face the schoolwork I had put off all weekend and then go for a long run, Sexy Sue and Passionate Paula on my mind.

Chapter 22

Outdoor Stories

> Drunk and spunky, J.C. and I decided to try
> and convert the poor heathens to our one true
> faith. I felt qualified to do so, given my
> commitment to the Lord, my growing leader-
> ship responsibilities, and my familiarity with
> evil in its many forms.

My family never left town. Our annual family vacation consisted of a trip to Kings Island, an amusement park. We'd spend the night in a nearby hotel, enjoying the amazing luxury of air conditioning as well as an indoor *and* outdoor swimming pool. To this day, strong chlorine and that antiseptic hotel odor smell like a good time to me.

I envied those families who journeyed somewhere far away every year: the Grand Canyon, Yellowstone, Yosemite. I dreamt of wide, open places, tall trees, and glimmering mountaintops, the opposite of my largely brick, concrete, and asphalt world.

Life was better outside. Streaking. Youth group picnics. Drive-in movies. Nature was pure and godly, the only "place" that even approximated the beauty of St. William's Church. As refreshing as I found Rapid Run and the other small parks in my neighborhood, I just assumed that both the majesty and the therapeutic effects of, say, the Rocky Mountains, would prove much more potent. A breath of real mountain air; a toe dipped in a cold trout stream; a glance of an elk or moose in the wild. All of it would do wonders for me.

While a national park wasn't within reach, a state park was. J.C. and I often camped at Hueston Woods just thirty miles north of town. We hitched rides from older friends or from one of our brothers.

For me, the allure of camping was the fresh air punctuated with the smell of burning wood, as well as the dark sky packed with more stars than I could see at once.

Though my faith had me feeling invincible on most days, there were others when I felt that my days were slipping away fast. If God were really on my side—if God *were*, period—I wouldn't be carrying this burden. Not for this long, anyway. On those days of doubt, nothing would reassure quite like the night sky ablaze. God was up there. I was sure of it. Or at least pretty sure of it. I told myself that someday, somehow, all of this would make perfect sense, if not down here, then up there.

Camping out also allowed J.C. and I to drink like sailors on shore leave without fear of puking our guts out at home, the wrenching noises alerting parents to our drunkenness. At the campground, J.C. and I would hide in the woods drinking our beer so as not to be spotted by a park ranger or a nosy, do-gooder camper. Once buzzed, we'd roam the campground looking for girls, though a watchful parent almost always seemed nearby.

On one trip we did find some girls our age camping solo. J.C. and I were both making progress until I decided to pee on their pup tent. I thought it a display of machismo. The girls saw it differently. J.C. laughed so hard that he didn't hassle me for spoiling what could have been a good time.

J.C. and I didn't even bother to bring a blanket, let alone a tent. We usually slept on the picnic table allocated to our camping spot or, when old enough to drive, in his car. When roaming the campground on one trip, we noticed a group of about fifty people, adults and children, under a campground shelter. They appeared to be laughing and having fun. We approached to investigate. To our delight and surprise, the strangers invited us to join them. After exchanging pleasantries, one announced that they were a New York chapter of a Buddhist association. Surprising, I thought at first. None were baldheaded. None wore robes.

Drunk and spunky, J.C. and I decided to try and convert the poor heathens to our one true faith. I felt qualified to do so, given my commitment to the Lord, my growing leadership responsibilities, and my familiarity with evil in its many forms. These goofy Buddhists had been led astray, no doubt by Satan himself. It was my duty to get them to see the error of their ways.

"Why do you worship false gods?" I said, after accepting some punch and a homemade chocolate chip cookie.

"Buddha is no false god, we can testify to that," said a middle-aged woman, with a friendly face and eyes that seemed content. She appeared to be the leader of this gang of unbelievers.

"I'm here to testify that Jesus is the one and only God," I said, tasting the punch like I sipped Jesus' blood in church.

"He may be *one* of them," she answered.

"I beg your pardon?" I said.

"Why can't there be more than one god?"

"There can only be one master," I said, thinking I pulled this from the Bible, but unable to recite chapter and verse.

"But don't you worship a *trinity* of gods: Father, Son, and Holy Spirit?" she said while crossing herself. Blasphemy!

"Damn straight."

"Well, by my count, that's *three* gods."

"But they're one. Three gods in *one*," I said, holding a finger near her face. "It's a mystery."

"I like that. Buddha is mystery."

"Buddha will lead you astray."

"We only lead ourselves astray," she said.

"No, ma'am," I said, shaking my head vigorously back and forth, "that's the Devil talking."

J.C. couldn't stop snickering in between puffs of his cigarette. "You can let go of the hippie thing," he said. "The sixties are over, lady."

"Buddha is for all time," the woman responded, a few of her followers nodding in agreement, the rest talking amongst themselves and playing cards, oblivious to—and ungrateful for—the wisdom J.C. and I were trying to share with them.

"Read the Bible," I said, putting my hands together and then pulling them apart as if to demonstrate opening a book. "You'll see the truth," I added, pointing to the stars.

"Buddha *is* the truth," the leader said.

"You're nuts," J.C. said, snickering.

"He's right, Buddha's nuts," I said.

"Open your mind to possibilities," the leader said.

J.C. and I could tell we were getting nowhere. These pagans were clearly not interested in truth, redemption, and holiness. Their punch was weak and their cookies chewy to boot. As we walked away, I turned my head and shouted my parting shot, one that I was sure was divinely inspired: "Believe what you want, fools! Jesus still loves you!"

If I were to encounter such a group today, I would be more interested in learning about its faith and what it holds in common with my own. One of my roommates in college was a Hindu. It was a joy getting acquainted with his worldview, and he seemed equally intrigued with mine. In exchange for helping him with his Catholic theology courses, he'd tell me about life in Katmandu, Nepal, and how his faith is lived there. We used to joke about how, on Fridays at least, neither of us would eat meat.

Everything was better outside. Running, making out with girls, even arguing. Certainly work was better outside, too. The summer before my sophomore year, I joined the Youth Conservation Corps and helped maintain a new, thirty-acre nature preserve in Price Hill called Glenway Woods. Our base of operations was a public elementary school on the edge of the preserve. The fifteen kids on the crew came from all parts of the west side. Some were even Protestants. Most kids were dropped off by parents in spiffy station wagons. Some, including myself, traveled by city bus to our day of manual labor.

The YCC program included a bit of instruction on how to care for the tools we were using, tips for identifying native flora and fauna, and some basic first aid training. But mostly we worked building trails, protecting wildlife habitat, and assisting with erosion control. As we shoveled, picked, and raked, we swapped stories, told jokes, and teased one another. I earned a reputation among my fellow trail builders for telling tall tales and, especially, for making excuses when the supervisors thought we hadn't made enough progress for the day.

"Well, you see," I explained to our young adult team leader, "the grade of this hill, easily a 7.5 on the McFarmington Scale, is such that work must progress slowly. If any one of us were to shovel too fast, the whole darn hillside would come down. For their own safety, I urged my colleagues to proceed with the greatest caution today."

"Mr. Kissing, pick up your shovel and get your butt in gear," the leader said, forcing back a smile. "Or I'll dock your pay 7.5% percent, based on the McFarmington Scale."

As I swung a scythe or pumped shears at the nature preserve, I often pretended that I was blazing trails out in Yosemite or Glacier National Park, singing God's praises with each swing or pump, Satan too busy tormenting kids back East to be found in those beautiful, quiet places.

At Glenway Woods, Satan sometimes cut trail with me, spoiling the moment by jumbling things in my head. Branches turned to hubcaps. Birds became hunks of dirty ice. And the scent of gas, the leaded type, replaced honeysuckle.

When Satan visited, I would stop my work suddenly and inexplicably and just stare off as if I had spotted some rare bird in the sky.

"Are you all right?" someone would sometimes ask. But since we all took regular breathers in the thick Ohio humidity, my dazing off was easy to dismiss.

"It's just hotter than hell," I'd say, wiping my brow. "Hotter than hell."

After a day of building trails, I would join up with some of my Elder teammates and run five to ten miles in preparation for the coming cross-country season. To sustain the energy required for the trail work and the long-distance running, I consumed large numbers of calories, though my build stayed just slightly above stick thin. Every morning as we young conservationists gathered for the ceremonial flag-raising, I ate an entire box of Pop-Tarts, washed down with an icy cold Coke.

To celebrate the end of the summer and our good work, we corps members held a backyard grill-out at Ann Tulley's house, a Seton student. After a picnic meal and some water balloon and egg-toss games, each person was presented with a paper plate on which a prediction was written by fellow coworkers. For instance, on the plate given to Lenny Boot, a good-looking kid with perfect teeth from the paneled-basement set, someone wrote: "Lenny will become a fashion model and then star in a soap opera." Mine read: "We predict that Steve Kissing will become president of a Pop-Tart factory and bullshit his way out of any major problem."

I couldn't have been more pleased. The group clearly recognized my leadership skills. And I did seem to have the creative imagination to handle almost anything.

Almost.

A testament to my "storytelling."

Chapter 23

A Fork in the Road

I looked down at the floor and pleaded for time to speed up. Maybe my coaches would understand if I could lay it out for them: My salvation lay in good works rather than good times, in prayers rather than pavement pounding, in the Bible rather than the record books.

By late August I was ready to get back to school and start my sophomore year. School meant an enhanced social calendar: Friday night football games, Saturday night dances, and Sunday night youth club meetings.

Better still were the Saturday morning cross-country meets.

My freshman track season the previous spring was a real letdown. My best mile run time was just five minutes flat, only seven seconds faster than I ran as an eighth grader. While I always ran better on the longer, hillier cross-country courses than on the flat, quarter-mile track, I was nonetheless disappointed.

Fearful that I was somehow losing my edge, I grew even more serious about my running that summer. In addition to tossing who knows how many shovelfuls of dirt and "manure" at the nature preserve, I logged more than 750 miles, an average of eight miles every single day.

At that point I had passed the two-year mark without missing a single day of running.

I won several races my sophomore year, during which the official racing distance was increased from two miles to two-and-a-half miles. I even qualified for the varsity team. Given the cross-country tradition at Elder (and the fact that only seven guys comprised a "team"), making varsity as a sophomore was something worth bragging about. It also meant that I earned the honor of exchanging my purple warm-up suit for the white version worn by the varsity.

I was in heaven. And dressed in white. Perfect.

My first varsity race was the Tiffin Invitational, a big meet two hundred miles north of Cincinnati. It was the furthest I had been from home. Unaccustomed to running in the middle of the pack—though not a bad place for a sophomore in a group of upperclassmen—I ran poorly. I finished last for the team, covering the two-and-a-half mile course in 14:14. In my race log, I drew an upside-down arrow next to my time and wrote the word "choke."

Head Coach Glenmary sent me back to the reserve squad. I wasn't that disappointed, though. I preferred to be back running up front where the glory was. In one of my best races of the season, just a week after my disappointing varsity race, I covered a three-mile course in 16:42, placing second out of 160 runners.

Another bonus to my sophomore season was that J.C. ran on the freshman team, at one point even making its "Top Seven." This was an impressive achievement given that J.C. smoked more than an occasional cigarette. "You can't smoke 'em if you don't smoke 'em," J.C. often said.

For me, the biggest race of the year was, of course, the city-wide Catholic school championships. I won them as a freshman and, therefore, had a title to defend on my home course at Rapid Run Park. I figured Jesus, and the Devil, paid more attention to this race given the religious significance of it. An all-Catholic meet had to matter more since there were no Protestants or Jews—and certainly no Buddhists—to somehow complicate matters or, worse, steal a victory.

The Devil wanted me to lose, of course. I expected him to interfere somehow. Maybe he'd cause me to trip. Or send a gut-splitting cramp. Or curse me with diarrhea. As I was warming up, the Devil did indeed come calling. Not once but *twice*. The first visit happened about thirty minutes before the start of my race, the second just a few minutes before the starter's gun went off. I would rather have been pooping in my pants.

In the first episode, a tree took on the image of a rifle, the leaves on the ground registered in my mind as frozen ice treats. In the second episode, yellow school buses that brought the various teams to the park registered as giant-sized hammers. People turned into factory smokestacks. In both episodes the noise inside my head was intensified by parents and teammates shouting encouragement to those running in the freshman race. The headache interfered with my prerace ritual: a series of prayers asking for the peace of mind to focus on the race and to kill the competition. I always spent the last few minutes before a race off by myself, sometimes mumbling encouragement to myself, so no one noticed my little mental recess.

Dad filmed the better part of that race on his silent movie camera. He missed the Devil's first visit, but he did capture me walking to the start line just moments after the second visit, my head down.

I was pissed that the Devil kept coming and that he tried to ruin my repeat victory at the Catholic school championships. I

Chasing a competitor on the cross-country
course at Rapid Run Park.

used this anger to propel me. When the starter's gun went off and
we fifty harriers dashed over hill and dale, I zoomed up front but
trailed Jimmy Klunk, my archrival from St. Ignatius, now running
for LaSalle High School. He led for the first mile-and-a-half, but I
took advantage of a quarter-mile long hill to seize the lead.

I covered the hilly two-and-a-half mile course in 13:50, winning by more than ten seconds. I considered that race and that
season my best to date. Come spring, I vowed to buck my personal trend and achieve similar results on the flat track. And I
mapped out a training schedule that would ensure success. My
plan was to run a thousand miles over the winter, even if I had to
run them all in my basement. Nothing would stop me. Nothing.

I was no longer a child, per se, but a young man who was old
enough to drive and hold down a job. But I wasn't smart or coura-
geous or articulate enough to approach a parent, teacher, or
priest to discuss the weird stuff in my head. My silence fed on itself, as secrets often do. The longer I went without saying anything, the harder it became to say anything. I still held out hope
that I could pray and "do good" my way out of my predicament.
And if I couldn't, I figured, I would eventually reach some sort of

breaking point at which time the world would come to know what had been happening to me. And who I *really* was. But my money was still on the power of prayer and penance. Besides, as with running, it did no good to look backward for you could easily lose a stride or two.

Right after the season ended, I began running five miles in the cold, dark mornings before school and another five to ten in the gray afternoons. On Saturdays and Sundays, I'd run ten to fifteen miles each day. The first three weeks went as planned. But then my right knee began to hurt. I slowed down for a couple of days and the pain subsided. But as I tried to build my mileage back up, the throbbing returned. But this time it didn't go away regardless of how slow or how little I ran.

Sitting at the dining room table one night doing homework, my right foot propped up on a chair and a plastic bag full of ice on my knee, I began to wonder if God were trying to tell me something.

My running demanded a lot of time and energy. I had proven that I could do it well. I had not, however, achieved anywhere near the same level of success with my leadership development. Perhaps it was time to redirect all my spare time and energy toward my church activities.

How was I best to use my skills and talents—those of distance runner and those of youth leader? What would please Jesus the most? What would shove the pitchfork back in the Devil's face?

I rubbed my red, slightly inflamed knee, the skin clammy, and decided that this tough question had to be answered. Soon. Time was awasting.

In my prayers, I praised God for my running but also for my calling to church leadership. I asked for some help in making the decision, and upon my request an idea came to me. I told God that I would run after school the next day. If my knee hurt, I would interpret that to mean that I should stop running competitively and get more involved in the church. If my knee didn't hurt, I would continue to run for his glory.

The next day I ran two miles, gingerly and just barely. My knee hurt so bad that I didn't so much run as shuffle.

God had spoken.

A few days later, I conjured up the courage to walk into Father Gest's classroom right after school. He served as an auxiliary chaplain of the cross-country team. He was a handsome man, one with a face that could look warm and inviting and then, in a matter of moments, turn mean and menacing. A perfect face for a high school teacher, I thought. I stepped softly into his class that afternoon, in a way hoping he wouldn't even notice me and just keep grading the papers on his desk.

Father Gest asked what was on my mind and I told him of my decision. He just nodded and told me I had to follow my heart. And then, much to my horror, he called Mr. Lanmeyer, one of the teachers who volunteered time in the athletic department, into the classroom. I was planning on telling the athletic director or Coach Glenmary the next day. Or maybe the next week. No doubt Mr. Lanmeyer would tell them right away. Ugh.

"Go ahead, Steve," Father Gest said, sitting on the edge of his desk. I was sitting on a chair next to him. Mr. Lanmeyer was standing in the doorway. He must have picked up a vibe that some bad news was coming because he had a hand on each side of the doorway, bracing himself.

"I've decided to stop running for the Purple Pack," I said looking at Father Gest rather than Mr. Lanmeyer.

"What?" Mr. Lanmeyer said, his voice cracking while he shifted his weight.

"I've decided to do other things."

"What things?"

"Leadership things. Church things."

"Church things?" Mr. Lanmeyer said, confused. How could God in any way interfere with athletics?

I forced myself to make eye contact with him. He wore one of those "this is some sort of joke, right?" looks. He had been one of the cross-country team's biggest supporters over the years. The looks we exchanged were like those of girlfriend and boyfriend breaking up.

"He's very involved in his church youth group," said Father Gest.

"He can do both," Mr. Lanmeyer said to Father, as if *I* weren't sitting there. "The coaches are going to be very disappointed in this news." He shook his head. I lowered mine. "You've been showing a lot of promise. And the coaches have been very good to you." They had been. They were men passionate about the sport and quite inspirational.

They had been. The coaching staff was first-class. I knew losing one of their top runners wouldn't please them. But there were others on the team who were really coming along. The team's future was bright without me.

Coming to my rescue, Father Gest said, "He doesn't think he can do both."

"I like to do things all or nothing," I said, trying to talk to Mr. Lanmeyer in his own "give it everything you've got" lingo.

"I'm sure the coaches can work around your schedule."

"I'll have things to do *every day* after school and on most weekends." I could have blamed my decision on my sore knee, but I knew that they'd send me to all kinds of sports doctors who would likely tell them that my knee was fine, just overworked, or, if it were more serious, that it could be repaired surgically.

"We can work it out," Mr. Lanmeyer pleaded.

"Apparently, he doesn't *want* to," Father Gest said.

I looked down at the floor and pleaded for time to speed up. Maybe Mr. Lanmeyer and my coaches would understand if I could lay it out for them: My salvation lay in good works rather than good times, in prayers rather than pavement pounding, in the Bible rather than the record books. But I dared not say such things.

Mr. Lanmeyer left, a bit dazed. He had no clue this news was coming. "Sorry," I said as he walked out. I inhaled deeply and exhaled as if I had just finish running a race.

Father Gest followed Mr. Lanmeyer out into the hallway. I could hear some mumbling. I stayed put, not sure what to do. Father Gest came back in a couple of minutes later. "You have to follow your heart," he said again. He grabbed some files and excused himself to attend a meeting. I sat in his office for a minute, at once relieved I had made a decision and also panic-stricken. Perhaps I had done the wrong thing. Running was as much as who I was as the 'Fro on top of my head. And I just put an end to the running part of me.

This CYO stuff better work out, I thought to myself.

After that ordeal, I hopped a bus and headed downtown to the diocesan youth office to help fold and label some newsletters. On the bus ride back home, I decided to lay my decision on Mom and Dad and just get the whole mess over with. At the dinner table, I poked at my food, rearranging pieces on the plate. I waited until my siblings had finished and walked away.

"There's something we need to talk about," I said, looking down on my salmon patties covered in ketchup.

"Well, spit it out," Mom said.

"I quit the cross-country team today." I braced myself for the worst: endless questions from Mom, God knows what from Dad.

"How come?" Dad said in a voice way too calm to be his at this moment.

"I want to do more with the youth group. I don't have time to do both things. Not the right way anyway."

"Did you tell someone at school?" Mom said.

"Yeah, just today."

"How did they take the news?" Dad said, sipping some carrot juice.

"Pretty well, I guess," I said.

"I doubt that," Dad said, laughing. Laughing! He wiped some carrot pulp off his lip.

"We want you to be happy," Mom said. "Take some time off and do those youth group things."

"Maybe you'll get the itch to run again," said Dad.

"Maybe," I said. I wanted to get away while I was ahead. "I best get to my homework."

I really thought that I might get a lecture from Dad. I anticipated hearing about how I was letting a team down, giving up on my talent, being a quitter. But Dad was cool with my decision. Even after the beer. That night I thanked God for leading me. I thanked God for my parents, for not pressuring me, for not second-guessing me. And I prayed that my coaches wouldn't corner me and give me endless grief. They were disappointed, but they didn't beat me or anything.

Life is full of surprises, I learned again that week. And the biggest ones were about to come.

Chapter 24

The Clash of Titans

> After all this time expecting the end to come,
> here it was. The good news: there was no fire,
> no screams of the damned. The bad news: no
> bright lights or angels playing harps. Maybe
> this was limbo, purgatory, or some sort of
> holding area.

Even though I quit the cross-country and track teams, I continued to run a couple of miles each day, out of habit, out of a desire to stay in touch with Dad, and out of fear that maybe I would change my mind, especially since my knee wasn't hurting anymore.

Running was a good friend, one I couldn't abandon overnight like an old pair of shoes. A few months later, though, finding it harder and harder to find the time, I stopped. My streak reached 1,080 days, just a bit shy of three years. I estimated that during that time I ran in excess of six thousand miles, enough to reach from Cincinnati to Rome, with plenty of miles to spare.

Quitting the track and cross-country teams surprised many people, especially my fellow students at Elder. Why go out when you're winning? Some thought that a college scholarship may even be in my future. (I knew that was unlikely, at least to a great college running program. I was no national stand-out. Not by a long shot.) Later in my high school career, I wrote an editorial for the school newspaper, The *Purple Quill*:

What would four high school years be without participation in sports? It's unfortunate that many here would answer: "A waste of time." I challenge that belief. . . . When one of my fellow students approached me to ask why I wasn't running this year, I responded that I have become involved in other things. Then he asked, "Are you into drugs"? . . . But sports aren't the only worthwhile thing on which to spend your high school years. High school life should not be restricted to the classroom or the playing field."

When it came to the social hierarchy at school, I was no longer sure where I fit. I wasn't an athlete, though I had been a decent one. I wasn't a burn-out, because I didn't smoke. I was, instead, some sort of Catholic youth leader. No one messed with me. I assumed that's because my classmates were afraid of Jesus, or they just found me too quirky to worry about.

They didn't know the half of it.

Some of this courage came from God, I believed. I saw him more as friend than father at this stage and thought we had a pretty good relationship. My prayers were less likely to be the old standbys, the "Our Fathers" and "Hail Marys" and such—though I still uttered a Grand Trilogy now and then. But I was more apt to try to engage God in dialogue, offering up my thoughts and ideas, hoping to make sense of what I heard in return. Years later I would appreciate that, at this point, the church was in full post-Vatican II swing. People were encouraged to feel comfortable praying to God without reciting prayers from memory or a prayer book. We were even permitted to go to confession face-to-face, having an actual conversation with the priest rather than just spewing out the usual script along with the usual lists of bad deeds. I found the whole experience much more meaningful. It was a bit awkward, however, talking about some sins face-to-face, especially those having to do with girls.

As my profile as a youth leader grew, I was occasionally asked to give witness to the Lord or share my feelings about the church. At one retreat—for mothers and grandmothers at St. William—my twenty-minute reflection included the following observations on Mass and Holy Communion: *Because of the blessings that Christ has given me, my family, my friends, St. William's Parish, the Elder community, and this world, there is just no way I couldn't attend Mass every week. I'd feel too guilty the next day . . . .*

I think the High Masses are really neat with all the candles, robes, and incense, but I think at times people forget that Christ is on that altar and in the church. I think God deserves that extra sign of praise and adoration. On the other hand, I've really enjoyed a couple of outdoor Masses with just a group of people sitting around the campfire really relating to Christ outside. . . .

Sunday Mass is my weekly "check-up" with God when I examine the week I just lived and ask for mercy toward my failings and for the support to conquer them in the next week . . .

I received my first Holy Communion way back in second grade. And my understanding of the Eucharist has changed drastically. I think second grade is way too early for kids to receive such an important sacrament. I think it's just too hard for them to comprehend that the little white thing is Jesus' body and that the wine—which makes Uncle Bob act goofy after family dinners—is actually the Blood of Christ.

The Eucharist has helped me cope with problems, settle personal conflicts, and prepare myself for the future. The Eucharist has strongly influenced my faith. The Body of Christ has the ability to put my mind at ease, to relax, and reflect on my own life. I wish more time were devoted to the Communion meditation during the Mass. I always have so much to think about and say to God.

The director of the retreat sent me a note afterward: "I sincerely believe your talk was one of the most inspiring parts of our weekend as your open expression of faith in such a natural manner is surely an example of what we need, hope for, and expect for the cause of Christ today and the future of God's church."

My Aunt Donna, Uncle Ken's wife, was an officer in the Child Advocate League. On behalf of her board, she invited me to address her club. She mailed me a typed, official-looking letter on club stationery. My topic: "Youth Attitudes Toward Religion."

A month or so later I stood inside someone's living room before Aunt Donna and fifteen others members as they sipped tea and coffee and nibbled on cakes and cookies. After delivering my thirty-minute presentation, I summarized my remarks with these points:

- If you consider religion important, then know it.
- Adjust your approach to your kid's age.
- Be prepared for questions.
- Don't feel you failed if your child looks into other religions.
- Communicate through words *and* actions.
- Believe in God and his will.

During the Q&A, one woman asked me how her troublemaker kid could connect more with Jesus. I pondered her question for a few moments, and then said: "Allow him to guide you. Remember that Jesus said to follow the example of children."

The woman nodded as if what I said made sense. She must have found me impressive. I know I did.

The fact that an adult would ask me such a serious question helped convince me that I had indeed risen to a position of authority. I was important. I could make a difference in people's lives.

To inform the world of my rank and status, I ordered some personalized stationery at the neighborhood quick-print shop. I had my name and address centered in red at the top of the page. I then asked the typographer to center the words "Youth Leader" underneath my name. All those I corresponded with—other youth leaders, priests, and girlfriends—would know I was gifted, talented, special. It said so in print.

One day, home alone in my bedroom, I wrote letters on my new stationery. I encouraged other youth

Stationery that spoke more to my arrogance than to my leadership.

group presidents to bring kids from their parish to St. William's next dance. The Devil interjected himself, however, and I couldn't get my hand to move. The visit seemed to last considerably longer, the voices louder, angrier. My poster of Bruce Jenner, arms up high in victory at the '76 Olympics, turned into a car? My third-grade homeroom teacher? Hitler? All of the above?

The last thing I remember was the sense of the whole world being covered in a shiny metallic blue paint, the kind used on toy cars.

The next thing I knew, I was facedown on the floor, blinking slowly as if coming out of sleep. My mouth was dry. My head was thick and heavy. The world was quiet, foggy.

I didn't move. Could I move?

My desk chair was on its side next to me. My nose was stiff. I tasted blood in my mouth.

Holy Christ! This was it.

After all this time expecting the end to come, here it was. The good news: there was no fire, no screams of the damned. The bad news: no bright lights or angels playing harps. Maybe this was limbo, purgatory, or some sort of holding area. It may all be over, but I had triumphed in any number of ways. I won races. I earned the right to put "youth leader" on my stationery. I had managed to get intimate with girls, including some really, *really* cute ones. And a few sluts, too.

I took a deep breath and pulled myself up from the bottom of my bed frame, my legs shaking. I sat on the edge of my bed and rubbed my head, which felt like it had been put through Dad's juicer. The sounds of the world—the real world, *this* world—began to filter back in. A bird chirp. A bus straining up the hill in front of our house. Mrs. Trentmen across the street calling for one of her kids.

I was still alive.

I assumed that I collapsed or fainted or something. I walked to the bathroom and splashed water on my face. My cheek was sore but not bruised. I lay down on my bed, shaking. My head hurt too bad to try to make sense of anything. Sometime later—minutes? hours?—my younger brother, Dave, ran upstairs into our room with a friend, startling me awake.

Did I dream what I thought had happened? An intense headache, stiff neck, and sore cheek couldn't be denied. I definitely fell on the floor. But why? How?

Either the Devil just kicked my butt or Jesus just kicked Satan's. It was a clash of the titans—good v. evil, pleasure v. pain, light v. darkness. And *Steve Kissing: Youth Leader* was caught in between. Something either very good or very, very bad just happened. I didn't know which. But I had a sense that I would know soon. Real soon.

Chapter 25

Chariot of the Gods

I went to bed dreaming I'd be the star of the show at brunch the next day—and win the trip to nationals. Little did I know that I would indeed become the star. The kind that collapses in on itself.

Scoring points with God reached a new level of urgency. If what happened in my bedroom was a bad thing, I needed big things—*good* things—to happen in a hurry. The timing was ideal. I was due to hear any day about who would be the Hugh O'Brian Award Winner at Elder.

One sophomore chosen from various high schools in Ohio would attend the Hugh O'Brian leadership conference. The best part of the Hugh O'Brian program is that one of the Ohio sophomores would be selected to represent our great state at the national conference in Anaheim, California. I couldn't have imagined a better reward.

One day in geometry class my guidance counselor, Mr. Bushman, knocked on the door and asked my teacher if I could step out for a moment. Mr. Bushman said that he wanted to personally deliver the good news: I was Elder High School's Hugh O'Brian award winner.

Hallelujah!

Since I wasn't running competitively, it felt especially good to taste victory again. I had even beat some paneled-basement kids out of the award. And this latest achievement would look good on my college applications a few years down the road.

I was especially thrilled with the all-expense-paid trip to Columbus where, during a three-day conference, I would meet a hundred other Hugh O'Brian leaders. Perhaps the Devil was communicating with one of them, too. I'd find out in just a couple of weeks.

Linda Morgan, the Hugh O'Brian winner from Seton High, invited me to ride to the conference with her and her parents. I gladly accepted, since Mom needed our car for work and I didn't want to have to take a Greyhound bus.

The Hugh O'Brian conference was held at a community college. The schedule included lectures on how to inspire other kids to get involved; sessions for honing organizational and public

The certificate proclaiming me the "Outstanding Sophomore" that I already knew I was.

speaking skills; discussions about world problems—everything from nuclear proliferation to gasoline shortages. We were confident that we could fix any, if not all, of these problems if only given the chance.

The evenings were filled with games, skits, and good-natured pranks. All of the activities, both the formal and the informal ones, were monitored closely by the adult moderators. They were keeping score. I knew it. Everyone else knew it. Only one of us would be sent to the national conference. If I won, and I thought I had a good chance at it, I decided that I would change my letterhead to read *"National* Youth Leader." And I would have these words printed in blue, a serious color, and one that would then give my stationery a red-white-and-blue look befitting a young American leader.

I played nice with all the other Hugh O'Brian award winners. But I secretly made note of their weaknesses. She's not very bright. He doesn't speak very well in front of groups. He's obviously just a stupid jock. She's too uptight. He's got a nervous twitch.

I encouraged others, as leaders are supposed to do. But I also seized every opportunity to let others know that I was serious competition for that plane seat to the West Coast. "Hi, I'm Steve, what's your name?" I asked a pretty redhead in preppy clothes as we walked down the hall to another workshop.

"Melissa. Melissa Banks." We shook hands.

"Where you from?"

Melissa flashed me a button with her school's coat of arms. "St. John's High."

"Where's that?"

"Cleveland. Actually about fifty miles south."

That was enough small talk. It was time to go in for the kill. "So what kind of things are you involved in?" I asked.

"Band and the debate team, mostly. How about you?"

"I'm president of my parish youth group, which was named the best in the archdiocese last year. I'm also planning to run for chairman of the Cincinnati area CYO someday. I lead several committees at school, too."

"Wow, that's a lot."

"I try to do as much as I can," I said, trying my hardest to sound modest. "I'm also a two-time league cross-country champion, I'm involved with a dance marathon for the Muscular Dystrophy Association, and I'm chairing the decorations committee for the sophomore dance."

"Jeez, and I thought I had my hands full." I could practically hear the wind leaving her sails. How sweet the sound.

I participated in all the Hugh O'Brian conference activities, being sure to be seen by the official scorekeepers. I raised my hand during most every Q&A session, but I didn't make speeches or go off on tangents like some losers. I took the time to compliment the guest speakers after their speeches—and sure to be seen doing so.

During breaks we took walks around the community college and played some volleyball. I picked up litter, not like an environmental nut on a crusade, but instead just a piece here and there, casually, as if it were second nature. If someone tripped, I offered a hand. If someone sneezed, I was sure to say "God bless you." I would have been doing most of this anyway, but I wouldn't have done it as often, or with as much gusto, if so much weren't on the line. My letterhead should have read "Steve Kissing: *Manipulative Youth Leader*."

The pressure mounted when, on Saturday afternoon, the conference organizers posted the name of the ten finalists. A panel would interview these ten. One would walk away with the trip to California at the Sunday farewell brunch.

I made the short list.

I brushed my teeth—and my 'Fro—before the interrogation. I said the Grand Trilogy, three times. When I entered the small library for my interview, I paced while waiting my turn. I reminded myself to be all smiles—and careful to say "sir," "ma'am," "please," and "thank you." When my name was called, I walked to the back of the room where four adults, seated behind a table, welcomed me and then tossed questions my way.

"Where do you see yourself in ten years?" a woman asked, tapping her pencil against her clipboard.

"I see several possibilities, but whether I'm a priest, businessman, or a politician, I expect to be involved with helping to make our world a better place." I gave myself credit for cleverly working in the priesthood, while also demonstrating ambition by mentioning "businessman" and "politician," too.

"What's the biggest challenge facing young people today?"

"Apathy. Too many just don't seem to care." I, on the other hand, cared. A lot. I was the epitome of caring.

"What can be done about that apathy?"

"Demonstrate the power of involvement by example."

"Who are some of your heroes?"

"President Kennedy, Bruce Jenner, Archbishop Joseph Bernadin, and Paul McCartney." I anticipated this sort of question. So I was ready with an answer that included several prominent Catholics, as well as a gold medal winner and the greatest rock musician of all time. I was one hip kid.

I thought I handled the interview well, but not great. I had not anticipated some of the questions: *What* practical *thing can you do today to improve the world? How might you motivate someone to work harder for a better world?*

I knew I would have to make something happen with the talent show that night. But what? I couldn't sing. I couldn't dance. I didn't play an instrument.

Quickly, I put together a stand-up routine of clean jokes, the kind I usually didn't tell or appreciate hearing. I even borrowed some material from my eighth-grade talent show routine.

I rehearsed a few times in my dorm room, double-checked my 'Fro and then high-tailed it down to the cafeteria for dinner. The talk at the tables was largely on who was going to win the California trip. A few people publicly declared that they thought *I* would. I feigned disbelief. But not too much. This dinner table vote was encouraging, but not particularly meaningful, since no adults were within earshot to hear that I was clearly the People's Choice.

After dinner we were ushered to the theater for the talent show. A few young ladies sang, some tap-danced. Some guys played instruments, one performed magic tricks. One girl read some poems about falling leaves and melting snow. One boy told a scary campfire story. They were all pretty good.

I then took the stage and told my cheesy jokes. I began by asking the audience: "How do you make a tissue dance?" Short pause. "Put a little boogie in it." This and my first couple of jokes garnered a few chuckles, mostly from the adults who, I hoped, valued the simple, old-fashioned humor. After a couple of more jokes, I was almost booed off stage. I left on my own accord before there was no doubt about whether I was pushed or jumped. I nonetheless thought I made the right decision by performing. I was hoping the adults would at least appreciate the gallant attempt. Real youth leaders don't just sit there.

I went to bed dreaming I'd be the star of the show at brunch the next day—and win the trip to nationals. Little did I know that I would indeed become the star. The kind that collapses in on itself.

At the farewell brunch the following morning, we youth leaders listened to a few "You are the future of America" speeches while we were served our meal. I panicked. Despite all my efforts to win the big trip, I had failed to consider an acceptance speech. How dumb of me! Since by this time the votes were already in, I didn't have to worry much about what impression I made on the seven other youth leaders and two adult moderators at the table. So I withdrew into myself and began composing my remarks: *I appreciate this wonderful honor. I didn't expect to win given the many terrific and talented youth leaders gathered here. You can rest assured, however, that I will represent the great state of Ohio to the best of my ability and do the Buckeye State proud.*

A waiter snapped me out of my speechwriting exercise when he reached over my shoulder and placed dessert in front of me, a small white dish of lime ice cream. I had a flashback to the extended family of gerbils I'd murdered in cold blood and then buried in an ice cream container. I still had not told anyone—*anyone*—about the rodents I murdered. And, as if on cue, Satan came calling. A veteran of hundreds of episodes at this point, I just told myself to ride it out. And I hoped with everything I had that the Devil and Jesus wouldn't start throwing punches again.

The last thought I recall having was of a fellow teenage leader registering in my mind as my Grandpa Elmer. The world turned a metallic color again, this time red. A wild, primordial scream ricocheted within my skull and a powerful charge—not unlike the one I received years earlier from the alarm clock—shot from my head to my toes.

Then total darkness.

Nothingness.

Death?

The next thing I knew I was coming to in brightly lit room, full of white and chrome, a slow back-and-forth rocking motion gave me the sensation that I was moving. But where? Was this a chariot of the gods?

After a few more head shakes and eye blinks, I could see that I lay on a stretcher, yellow canvas belts strapped over my torso and legs. A man with a light blue shirt with a red cross came into view. He was sitting on a jumpseat and leaned over to ask how I was.

I didn't answer. I didn't know.

The man said we were in an ambulance on our way to Children's Hospital.

Oh, my God!

Our father, who art in heaven, hallowed be thy name . . .

Chapter 26

Bumbling Idiot

Other, potentially more ugly and violent signs

were sure to come. Soon I would grow horns

and speak in gargled grunts. Soon I would be

expelled from the Catholic Youth Organiza-

tion. Soon no girl would want to kiss me.

As I gained my bearings in the ambulance, I noticed that an adult chaperone from the conference, Mr. Perry, was along for the ride. Mr. Perry, about sixty-five, kept shifting back and forth in his seat. He explained calmly that I had some sort of seizure at the banquet. I would be okay, he said, in a manner that was intended to be reassuring. But I wasn't buying it. I knew better.

I would learn later that I grunted real loud, flopped off my chair, and started doing a horizontal jig. My eyes rolled to the back of my head while half-eaten bites of lime sherbet oozed out of my mouth. (The similarity of this true-life scene to those in the movie *The Exorcist* left many a dessert at the conference uneaten.)

I began to cry. And I cried harder when I realized that this blew my chances for the trip to the national conference. How could I possibly represent the great state of Ohio while flipping around on the floor, oozing and grunting? Ohio is, after all, the "Buckeye," not the "Bug-Eyed," state.

Mr. Perry told me again that everything would be okay. But the poor guy had no idea what he just witnessed. Nor that he and the EMTs were escorting one of the Devil's own—to a children's hospital no less. Forgive them, God, I thought, for they know not what they do.

Upon arrival at the hospital, the EMT pulled me out of the ambulance and wheeled me into an examining room where I was shifted to a bed. I lay there for a few moments, still wondering if perhaps I was dreaming. I lifted my head high enough to spot Mr. Perry talking to a doctor in the hallway. After a few minutes, and a brief demonstration by Mr. Perry about how I fell on the floor, the handsome young doctor, with eyes even brighter than TM tutor Lester, walked in and introduced himself.

"I'm Dr. Tierra." He shook my hand firmly and smiled.

"Hi," I said.

"How do you feel?"

"My head really hurts. *Bad*."

"Anything else?"

"My neck is stiff and my legs are sore."

"So what happened?" he asked, one hand up to his chin, the other fiddling with his stethoscope.

"I'm not sure."

He paused as if he were waiting for me to change my mind and tell him what he wanted to hear. "This kind of thing happen to you before?"

"No, but I got a funny feeling right before it did."

"What do you mean?"

"Weird things in my head. It's kind of hard to explain." What was I supposed to say? That I saw Peter Frampton sitting next to me? Call the psych ward!

"I see," the doctor said, scribbling notes in my chart, nodding as if what I just told him made sense. "Well, let me take a look." He aimed his pen light into each of my eyes. He then had me sit on the side of the bed while he poked and prodded me some, and checked my reflexes. He then asked me to bend and twist my neck.

"Uh, hmm," he said, several times, picking up the chart and jotting more notes. What the guy could be writing, I didn't have a clue. I wasn't saying anything.

"So this has never happened before?"

"No." I sounded a bit more abrupt than I had intended, but I was dying, or at least my spirit was, right in front of him.

"Can you tell me more about these weird things in your head?"

I was too tired to fight any more. I decided to come clean. Exorcism and a mental institution were in my future. And truth was, at that point, I didn't much give a damn. I explained how I saw normal things that my mind told me were something else, how I heard voices, smelled gasoline, and saw, actually *felt*, colors.

"How long has this been going on?"

"I don't know," I said, wringing my hands. "A long time."

"Months?"

"More than that."

He paused again, shaking his head. "A year?"

"Years." I said. The doctor's eyes lit up. "*And years*," I added, looking down.

"Your parents know about this?"

"No."

"Anybody know?"

"Nope." I just shook my head and hunched my shoulders as if to say I was just as surprised as he was.

"So you're not on any medicine?"

"No. *None*." I thought doctors were supposed to be smart. This guy wasn't getting it.

A nurse walked in with some water and graham crackers. The doctor called my parents from a phone in the room. I heard the doctor explain to my Dad that I'd had a seizure. I could overhear Dad protesting through the earpiece. The doctor must have been mistaken. Surely there was another Steve Kissing in the room, for the Steve Kissing Dad knew couldn't have had a seizure. Not possible. He's healthy as a horse, gets good grades, and is president of his youth group.

The doctor held the phone up and aimed it toward me. I shouted hello to Dad. He stopped arguing. The doctor said there was no need for my parents to come up to Columbus. The best thing would be for me to hitch a ride home to Cincinnati with the family who brought me. Once home, I could see a neurologist who would likely want to admit me to a hospital for testing.

Mr. Perry made arrangements for Linda Morgan's parents to drive by the hospital with my luggage.

Despite the drugs I'd been given, my head still hurt. On the ride home, Linda kept chatting, I assumed, to keep my mind off what had just happened. That was fine by me. It wasn't like I wanted to spill my guts or anything. Besides, I figured her parents would make me hitchhike home if they knew they were transporting Damien back to town.

About midway home, flat farmland on either side of I-71, I finally got around to asking Linda what I wanted to know from the moment I stepped into her car.

"Who won the trip to California?"

"Some girl from up state. Laura something or other."

"Did she have an acceptance speech?"

"Yeah, she basically thanked God, her parents, and her school."

"That's good," I said, not sounding the least bit sincere.

"I thought you were going to win it."

"Me, too." I was too tired to hide my true feelings. "I suppose the commotion at the banquet didn't help me any."

"Oh, I'm sure *that* wasn't the reason. That girl seemed pretty sharp. I mean, not as sharp as you, of course, but on the ball."

"Didn't seem that way to me," I said in a soft voice, staring out the window. I wondered if perhaps I was slated to win the award and was nixed at the last moment when I crashed to the floor. Maybe it was time for my letterhead to read: *"Steve Kissing: Bumbling Idiot."*

When I walked inside my house two hours later, my head still pounding, my parents greeted me as if I had been away for years. Dad had a heavy look on his face, Mom was in tears. She jumped to the conclusion that I had a brain tumor. In Mom's embrace, I began to cry, too, assuming this was just the first visible clue that the Devil owned me.

Other, potentially more ugly and violent signs were sure to come. Soon I would grow horns and speak in gargled grunts. Soon I would be expelled from the Catholic Youth Organization. Soon no girl would want to kiss me.

The mood at home that evening was upbeat, no doubt a deliberate attempt to make me feel better and keep me, keep us all, feeling positive. The phone rang at least a dozen times, friends and family checking in. The word was spreading fast. I knew it would. Bad news always does. My family and friends seemed prepared to take up arms in this battle over my health. Of course they couldn't know that it was a holy war.

In bed that night, I wept more, my head still hurting.

I wanted to see Jesus in person someday. But not then. Or anytime soon.

Chapter 27

A River of Lies

My mind was now in a box. And inside that box sat a crazy story, *my* story. Was it over? Or just beginning? Perhaps I would need a head transplant like my brother Dave supposedly had after birth?

The day after my collapse in Columbus, I visited St. Francis-St. George Hospital with my parents for my neurological tests. I found it doubly reassuring that my head was being examined in a Catholic hospital named after *two* saints. I walked in with Mom and Dad still believing that I didn't really need a neurologist with brain-scanning devices, but rather a priest with some anointing oils. It may take a while, I thought, but eventually everyone will come to understand the true nature of my condition. It was just a matter of time.

We first sat down with a nurse's aide who asked me to describe what had been happening. I explained that immediately before the seizure in Columbus I had a weird feeling, one I had felt hundreds of times over the past six years. She looked at me and then my parents, her gaze scorning and quizzing them at the same time.

"We didn't know," Mom interjected with an understandably defensive tone.

"That's right," Dad added. "He didn't tell us. He didn't tell *anyone*."

The woman then aimed her slightly upturned nose—and her scorn—my way. I shrugged. She pulled a blood pressure monitor from a desk drawer. "Let's check," she said, while wrapping the cuff around my arm. "You know, some very famous people had seizures."

"Like who?" I asked, most anxious to know in whose company I now traveled.

"Socrates and Julius Caesar," she said. I must not have looked impressed, because she added, "And others."

"Hmm," Dad said.

"That's not what killed them, is it?" Mom said with a half laugh.

"Of course not," the nurse said, shaking her head at what she perceived to be a joke in bad taste. I thought it was funny.

What wasn't the least bit funny, however, is that I knew my parents didn't have a young Socrates or Caesar on their hands, but rather a young Son of Sam currently disguised as a mild-mannered youth leader. Surprise!

My doctors prescribed two tests: an EEG to check my brain waves and a CAT scan to take a picture of my brain.

For the EEG, a technician glued some thirty electrodes to my head. This took about twenty minutes. My furry 'Fro certainly made the job a bit more challenging. Multicolored wires protruding from the electrodes hung off the back of my head, where they merged into a psychedelic ponytail. The wires dropped to the floor and then wound their way to the EEG machine a few feet away.

I lay down on an examination table. The technician told me to lie still and keep my eyes open. I heard the EEG machine kick on, the hum of paper rolling underneath a row of electronic pens taking dictation from my brain. The EEG machine made me think of those devices that detect the lies of criminals. Of course, if I were connected to a lie detector, the machine would have gone haywire.

As I lay there, the pens scribbled away, creating a river of rickety lines in which swam my many stories, the made-up ones, like those I told at the nature preserve, and the real ones, like the ones I told God about my desire to live. And to keep kissing girls.

But would anyone really be able to read these stories? *Really* read them? Would these squiggly lines made possible by the marvels of modern science be able to detect Satan's presence? Or my desire to keep on living? To make something of myself? To keep kissing girls.

After about five minutes, the technician maneuvered a lamp near the examination table. She bent the flexible stand so that the bulb was positioned but a foot from my face. She told me to shut my eyes. She turned the bulb on. She explained that it would flash in a rapid-fire sequence. She returned to her chair near the EEG machine. The light bulb flickered, first slowly and then quickly. Though my eyes were closed, the light penetrated my lids, creating a psychedelic pattern of twirling, pulsating shadows that lasted for a few minutes. The machine clicked off and the electronic pens slowed to a halt.

On the floor sat a cardboard box that had collected pages and pages of my transcribed brain waves. My mind was now in a box. And inside that box sat a crazy story. *My* story. Was it over? Or just beginning? Would I need a head transplant like my brother Dave supposedly had after birth?

The technician just said "good" and helped me sit up on the table. With the help of a special solution, she removed the electrodes from my head. I was then wheeled to a waiting room where Mom and Dad sat, a seat apart, each staring at the wall.

I had to wait for about an hour, still in my hospital gown, before the CAT scan. I assumed that I had better get used to waiting. My days were soon to be full of this sort of thing: hanging out in institutions, wearing next to nothing, doing next to nothing.

"Did it go okay?" Mom asked, offering me a stick of gum.

"I guess so."

"Did the nurse say anything?"

"Not really. Just 'good.'"

"Just 'good'? Nothing else?"

"Nope."

Dad shook his head. He was clearly hoping for news. "How are you feeling?" he asked.

"I'm fine. My head hurts, but what else is new?" I said, scratching my scalp, the glue from the EEG itching like mad.

"Do you need something to eat or drink?" he asked.

"Maybe a drink."

"The technician said he shouldn't have anything before the CAT scan," Mom reminded Dad.

"Right. Sorry. I'll get you something later," Dad said. "I promise."

"Don't worry about it," I said. "I can wait."

A male nurse called my name. My parents were asked to wait while I was wheeled into another room for the CAT scan. I lay down on a plastic counter. An IV was connected to my arm. A bluish fluid, which the nurse warned may make me feel a bit unusual, was pumped into my arm. I could feel the fluid coursing through my veins and swirling around in my head. The cold counter I was laying on was then slid into the CAT scanning device, a tube of sorts.

The machine hummed and moaned. I felt nauseated. Alone with only my thoughts. And what do you think about when inside a device taking pictures of your brain? None of it is pretty: Tumors. Horrific pain. Drooling on yourself. Death. And, in my case, demons. I would have sworn that I heard them laughing, too. The CAT scan was over in about twenty minutes. I was wheeled back to my room, where Mom and Dad were already waiting, and where I would spend the night for observation.

My Uncle Ken and Aunt Donna visited, bringing with them a warm extra-cheese pizza from LaRosa's, precisely what I would have chosen if this were my last meal. As perhaps it was, at least the kind that I could feed to myself.

Other family members stopped by, as did some friends, including of course, J.C.

"You feeling normal?" he asked, holding two of my favorite things in the world: a *Mad* magazine and a bag of M&M's.

"A bit tired, but fine."

"What's this about stuff happening in your head and you not telling me, you jerk?"

"Yeah, hard to believe, eh?"

"What do the doctors think it is?"

"Seizures of some sort."

"What causes them?"

"Not sure, really," I said. "I'll find out tomorrow."

"You don't have a tumor do you?"

"Christ, I hope not."

"Yeah, me too," J.C. said, cracking his knuckles. "Would you like some beer?"

"Do you even have to ask? Of course. But I better not."

J.C. told me that an announcement was made at school that morning. The entire student body was informed that their Hugh O'Brian Youth Leader had fallen ill and was in the hospital for "brain tests." The principal asked the school to pray for me.

Prayers. Now that's exactly what I needed. A whole school asking God to help me. Amen!

"Well, try to get some sleep tonight," J.C. said.

Sleep? Tonight? Was he crazy?

J.C. walked out into the hallway, I watched my mom and dad quiz him. My parents were smart enough to know that if I told anyone, I would have told J.C. But they underestimated my ability to keep real secrets to myself: the gerbils I murdered, J.C.'s sister whom I lusted after, and of course, the Devil who chased me.

The night was long. Periods of restless sleep were punctuated by moments of intense anxiety, aggravated by odd buzzes, clicks, and murmured voices coming from other rooms on my wing. Or was I just imagining them? These periods were followed by spiritual moments, when I knew—as sure as anything—that God would win, that I'd be fine. These glorious thoughts were then chased away again by moments of shear terror, certain—beyond any doubt—that the Devil had already won.

It looked like the drunken nights, heavy petting, and stolen money had trumped my first place finishes, sincere prayers, and church activities. May Queens and holy water-soaked Wonder Bread weren't enough to save me.

I crossed and double-crossed myself three times.

The following morning, my mind tired, I began to question if the past forty-eight hours were even real. But they were. My parents and I met with one of several doctors working on my case, including one of the country's prominent neurologists. Each of these men and women had wonderful bedside manners. Each was cool, calm, and collected, just like you'd want a doctor to be. In addition to these physicians, I got some additional help from Dr. Patrick Kaplan. He typically practiced in New Mexico but was in town for a couple of years helping an ill friend manage his family practice. While in town he was also conducting some research of some sort about kids and brain problems. One man's curse was my blessing, for Dr. Kaplan had all sorts of cool brain models in his temporary office, and he wore an equally cool ponytail.

Dr. Kaplan asked me to repeat my story again: How did you feel right before the seizure in Columbus? How often had you felt that way before? How long has this been going on? You never once told anyone? Not a single person? Not a single time? "Interesting," he said. "Very interesting."

"He's always been an uptight kid," Mom volunteered.

I looked at Mom and raised my hands as if to say "gimme a break!" Spend your waking hours in fear of Satan—and insanity— and see what it does to *your* nerves, I thought.

What I found more interesting than my frayed nerves was how Dr. Kaplan and the other doctors were going to explain my condition. I sat still as he reviewed the tests results and proclaimed the diagnosis: what I had been experiencing all those years was a type of seizure, one in which the sufferer doesn't lose consciousness, but brain waves get all jumbled up and weird things happen in the mind. My big production in Columbus was a grand mal seizure, the fall-down-and-flip-like-a-fish-out-of-water type.

"That's fine," I said. "But what was the cause?"

"Well, we don't know for sure," Dr. Kaplan said. "The tests showed no significant abnormality."

But, of course! No machine could detect the Devil. Call in the chaplain. *Fast.*

"However," the doctor added, "my informed guess would be that there is a small scar, one we can't see, on your brain. It was probably caused at birth." I turned toward Mom, and she looked hurt, as if all of this was somehow *her* fault.

"Must have been *my* big head," I said, wanting to reassure her. "Good thing I wasn't born with my 'Fro."

"A head that big couldn't come out of an elephant," Mom said. It was good to hear her laugh.

Dr. Kaplan said that he and my other doctors believed that antiseizure medication would at least keep the grand mal seizures under control. I nodded on hearing all this—the good student and Catholic youth leader honoring authority. But I harbored doubts about any pill's ability to rid the Devil from one's system. If only.

Dr. Kaplan then advised my parents that I shouldn't drive until I was seizure-free *at least* six months. I thought immediately about the upcoming sophomore dance for which I chaired the decorations committee. I was hoping to escort my date, Joan George, a busty girl who could really dance, *alone*. Though I had my driver's license, neither I nor my parents could afford the insurance, so I didn't drive. But my Aunt Donna volunteered her car for the dance. I loved her for that. But unfortunately now I would have to double-date. Bummer.

Years later, I retrieved my medical records. When I did, I found this note that Dr. Kaplan had dictated after our initial meeting: *Steve Kissing is a sixteen-year-old gentleman seen in consultation because of seizures. History was obtained from the patient and his parents. For the past six years, Steve has been experiencing episodes characterized by a sudden onset of a feeling of unreality.*

During these times, he apparently is in semi-contact with his environment, but people and objects seem as if he has seen them previously in a dream. Familiar people seem unfamiliar, in a difficult to explain fashion. He is unable to answer questions during this time, and apparently he appears pale and sweats. . . . They usually last a minute or so and end abruptly without any definite post-event confusion . . . he is an excellent student, his health has otherwise been excellent, and he is a marathon runner.

215

On examination this morning he was pleasant, somewhat appre-hensive, intelligent, and articulate young man who gave a clear history . . . . The cause of Steve's seizures remain uncertain. . . . His prognosis for control of the generalized seizures should be good, though I am less optimistic in being able to control the minor seizures.

Dad drove us home in the Beige Bomber, my parents relieved that I didn't have brain cancer, I thankful that I now had some cover for my condition. Let the world think I had some sort of seizure disorder. No big deal. It was all a blessing. It bought me more time.

I made it to school the next day, students and teachers sharing their concern—and stories of dealing with me when I had one of my minor seizures.

"I remember once in history class, I was talking to you and then, like all of a sudden, you sort of spaced out or something."

"Now things makes sense. Once you were telling me a joke in study hall but you stopped midsentence and turned away. It was very freaky."

"I just assumed you were scatterbrained because of all the things you're into. I never took it personally."

"I called on you once in class and you ignored me. It was so un-like you, I had to call your name three times even though you were staring right at me."

I took it rather easy in school for the next couple of weeks. The year was winding down, and I figured that teachers would cut me some slack. I took my medicine every day even though I didn't expect it to matter.

Much to my surprise, the demonic visits stopped. A couple of weeks had come and gone without a single visit. Not one. And then a couple of months without an episode. Could I have been wrong? Could this really have been some sort of physical ailment? Some sort of little defect going all the way back to day one? I just couldn't believe it. At least not at first. Why would God make me suffer so?

I kept up my regimen of prayers, good works, and church leadership, in part because I had grown to like it all, feeling comfortable and secure in my personal relationship with Jesus and still believing that I was called to lead.

In addition, after six years of dodging the Devil, I feared dropping my guard.

It was a good thing that I didn't.

Chapter 28

A Backseat Calling

> I had built a world, indeed even chose and
>
> honed an identity that was dependent upon
>
> my special relationship with Light *and* Dark.
>
> Both wanted me. And in return, I wanted—and
>
> needed—them both, too. A Catholic carrot and
>
> a satanic stick.

Within days of starting my junior year, I wrote in my journal about the biggest moral albatrosses around my neck. There were three of them: drinking; girls; and masturbation. (Once again, Grandma Marge was right, *everything* meaningful did express itself three ways.)

I wrote that I needed to "cut my drinking by ninety-five percent." In addition, I noted that what little drinking I would allow myself to enjoy could only happen in secluded spots, like in a buddy's basement or backyard. That's so I wouldn't have to worry about making a fool of myself in front of my fellow young people whom I was allegedly leading. This had already happened on a couple of occasions, including once when I was found passed out in a bathroom stall at youth group dance. Steve

Kissing, youth leader, was found sitting on his throne, his head resting upon a roll of toilet paper. No one mentioned to me that alcohol wouldn't mix well with my medication since I wasn't old enough in the law's eyes to be drinking anyway. Even if something had been said, I doubt I would have stopped. I'm not sure I could have.

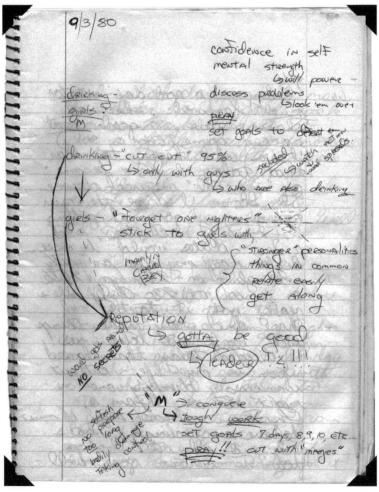

A page from my private journal.

I also noted in my journal that I should only drink with guys, since boozing it up in mixed company only seemed to whet my appetite for my second and third moral weaknesses.

As for girls, I wrote that I had to "forget one-nighters." I printed the names of four girls with whom I had made out even though I had no—and wanted no—long-term relationship. I put a big, red "X" over their names. I had to find and stick with those girls who met certain criteria, including strong personalities and common interests.

To help with my faith formation and leadership development, I had taken to corresponding with a couple of former CYO leaders who were then in college, the seminary, or early in their professional careers. One of these mentors, then living in New York City, wrote in response to my question about how he handled the burdens of being a CYO leader *and* a lady's man:

There are many gifts to be given in service to God. One of them is leadership. Being the main man in CYO places undue pressures on one's sexuality.

I often found myself living in two different worlds: one in the backseat of a car, one leading a prayer service. There was a profound contradiction in these two worlds. . . .

The world of physical passion, of banality and vice, is a very real world. It is a world of despair and loneliness, a violent struggle for union with others, a groping for the eternal. . . .

People are attracted to you because influence feeds on itself. You are placed at a vibrant, alive circle of friendship.

There is something pathological in power. I honestly believe it is rooted in a satanic drive to possess, to claim ownership of some of God's creation.

This last remark confused and worried me. I was seeking higher and higher offices to distance myself from Beelzebub. But my mentor was suggesting that perhaps I was doing the opposite.

220

It hurt to think about it, so I chose not to. Besides, with enough prayer and concentration, I figured I could, even in a backseat, escape the siren's call of "pathological power."

As for masturbation, I wrote in my journal that it was "selfish" and had "no purpose." Fighting masturbation was especially important in that, as I noted, it could lead to "bodily damage." I wasn't really worried about going blind so much as rendering myself impotent. On the other hand, I thought pleasuring oneself may make it less likely that something worse would happen. A friend of mine who went to public school told me that the mother of one of his Protestant friends encouraged him to masturbate before dates. That way, he would be less likely to get aroused and impregnate a girl. The Protestants never ceased to amaze me.

Overcoming these addictions was important, for I could not back away from my Devil-busting regimen. I feared Satan might return, especially since my doctors could not pinpoint the *exact* cause of my condition. And how could I change my mind now? I had built a world, indeed even chose and honed an identity that was dependent upon my special relationship with Light *and* Dark. Both wanted me. And in return, I wanted—and needed—them both, too. A Catholic carrot and a satanic stick.

Through all the cranial chaos, I couldn't see that this dependency on reward and punishment was perhaps my biggest addiction, my truest weakness.

Besides, I had grown so close to Jesus that I joined a program for high school boys considering the priesthood. This mostly entailed a couple of weekend retreats a year in which we potential priests hung out and prayed with actual priests and seminarians. We discussed things such as callings, counseling, and celibacy. I found everything but the celibacy part worth considering.

Interestingly and tellingly, I felt I received the call to the priesthood while snuggling with a girl in the backseat of a car. We were headed home after double-dating with J.C. and his girlfriend. This girl, her name was Becky McIntyre, was simply gorgeous. Like Mary Ann the May Queen, Becky was tall and had shiny green eyes. She also had a heart-melting smile that said, "hello," not "ain't I pretty?" Best of all, she had a lightning bolt tattoo on her left ankle. It made my insides thunder.

While Becky and I held hands and kissed in the backseat after the dance, I looked up through the rear window of J.C.'s car at a country sky sprinkled generously with stars. Countless angels up above, one next to me. There was only one way to pay back God: the priesthood.

Was I the first to hear the call of the Lord with an erection?

A few days later, I gave Becky a photo I purchased from a friend's brother that captured a beautiful sky painted with Monet's sensibilities. I placed the photo in a cardboard frame on which I wrote something that Abraham Lincoln allegedly once said: "I never behold the stars that I do not feel like I am looking in the face of God. I can see how it might be possible for a man to look upon the earth and be an atheist, but I cannot conceive how he can look up into the heavens and say there is no God."

Another reason why I felt called to the priesthood was my parents. Their marriage, I could tell, was losing steam. Mom didn't seem to joke with Dad nearly as much, and vice versa. Since my life was organized in such a way that I was seldom home except to sleep, I had lost touch with what home life was like for Mom and Dad. Dad continued to drink, though, and I knew that couldn't be good.

I was old enough to grasp in a basic way how difficult relationships can be. I had felt the pain of breaking up with girls after only months of dating. Mom and Dad had been together for nineteen years. On their anniversary, I wrote them a note of encouragement:

I hope your love is still as strong as the first day. Considering how young you were when you got married, your marriage has gone against all the statistics for how long it has lasted. I know both of you have given up a lot to provide for Larry, Dave, Teri and myself. We do appreciate it a lot. Keep working hard with us.

Family life was complicated, messy, and sometimes painful. I somehow thought I would be shielded from such heartbreak in the priesthood.

In a letter to Mom, I wrote: *When I think about my future, seventy-five percent of the time I think about it as a priest. I am at the stage now where I must begin to understand where I am at. I've gone out with many girls, some were respectable, others weren't. I do, however, remain a virgin.*

And about my seizures, if I ever have one and I get hurt or killed, I will hold no grudge, nor put the blame on anyone but realize that it's God's will. My attack was a test of my faith and your faith. Peace, Steve.

Another pen pal of mine, a young parish priest in Washington, D.C., whom I met at a retreat in Cleveland, wrote to help me figure out this girl/priesthood thing:

I can't believe you are dating Becky! She's wonderful! This is good for you and so important if you are serious about the seminary. Tell her you are thinking about going—perhaps sure *you are going—so that she knows just how close to get to you. Steve, watch yourself sexually, the slightest caress or petting makes a hell of an attachment for a girl. I know because I broke more than a few hearts.*

I'm glad you are responding to the call of the Lord; we need good men like you, but Steve, give yourself time. Don't be so sure that following his call means the college seminary. Keep taking time to pray daily and discern the spirit. Look over many options and decide when you must.

I really encourage as much seminary as possible for most guys who know what being drunk, getting a piece of ass, and the world is all about.

I especially liked that being drunk and piece of ass part. If that helped one prepare for the seminary, I was perhaps overqualified.

A month later I gave Becky a crucifix and told her of my calling. She took the news pretty well. She cried tears of joy. Then we made out.

I wasn't, however, prepared to get the news from my parents that we were moving out of Price Hill, to a bigger, better house in the suburbs, one we wouldn't have to share with another family. At this point, Mom was working for the youth court system at a group home. I assumed it paid more than her beautician gig, which is how she and Dad could afford a bigger home in the 'burbs.

Mom and Dad found a house in Bridgetown, about five miles west of Price Hill. I would soon be a member of St. Jude's Parish, a more modern and definitely less beautiful church, I thought. I was leaving Price Hill and joining the paneled-basement set. I wasn't sure which would be tougher to adjust to.

We moved down off God's Holy Mountain a month later. About three months after that I was back in the doctor's office. I had not had a seizure, but I explained to Dr. Kaplan how I just felt beat and sort of down.

Then Mom put her two cents in: "And he seems on edge most the time." I looked at her in complete disbelief. "We also found him sleepwalking on a couple of occasions."

"Is that so?" Dr. Kaplan said.

Dad, answering for me, nodded his head "yes" and added, "He's really moody, too."

Moody? Me? Imagine *that*, I thought. When I'm not worried about the Devil stealing my soul, I've got the world on my shoulders: leading my fellow young people, the very ones who are the teachers, priests, doctors, and, yes, the *parents* of tomorrow. Give me a break!

"Is your mom right?" Dr. Kaplan asked.

"Maybe a little," I said.

Dr. Kaplan lowered my daily dosage of antiseizure medication. In his notes from that meeting, he wrote: *Steve remains seizure-free. He has, however, undergone some change in personality according to his parents. Apparently, he sleeps during the day and has been 'moody.' He has lost some weight. . . . His neurological exam is normal. His school performance remains excellent. I suspect that these are changes unrelated to medication or seizures.*

The doctor was right about my mood. It wasn't *all* the medicine's fault. I missed my old neighborhood. I missed my old church. I missed Becky, who left me for another guy, one who wasn't thinking about the priesthood.

I also had this nagging thought that I couldn't shake: the doctor was also right about the cause of the seizures. It was something physical, *not* spiritual. Yet I couldn't accept that totally. If it were just physical, wouldn't God have sent a grand mal seizure earlier in my life so I wouldn't have thought it was something else? So I wouldn't have had to go to great lengths to hide my condition?

God wouldn't do something like that? Or would he?

It just didn't make sense.

Chapter 29

Losing Face

I was too cool and too blessed to wear a life
vest. Jesus was my life vest. But had the
Devil really socked one to me then, I could
have easily flipped in the water and drowned.
Unless, of course, Jesus was prepared to walk
on water again and offer me a helping hand.

In need of a job, I accepted an offer from a couple of CYO friends to get behind the counter at a local hamburger joint, Burger Beat. "Great place to meet chicks," one of them told me. I stopped by the restaurant and filled out an application. As I wrote, both of the adults behind the counter—the manager and assistant manager, I assumed—gave me the once-over. That was fine. I was certain that they could sense extraordinary integrity and reliability in my overall demeanor. It would be their pleasure to have me.

Several days later, my application processed, I was invited back for an orientation program. We new recruits were introduced to the virtues of cleanliness, speed, and courtesy. I—and I alone—was invited back the next day to meet the managers. I wasn't the least bit surprised. I assumed that my very presence in the orientation program was enough for them to see in me a leader of youth, of men, of double-cheeseburgers and fries.

Back the next day expecting to learn about the fast track to management, I was instead told by Tim Lanelle, Junior Assistant Manager, to cut my hair.

"It's way too long and, well, bushy," he said, raising his hands up to his head, each a foot from an ear.

"It worked fine for the Jackson Five," I said with a chuckle.

"But you won't see them cooking hamburgers. Not here anyway."

"I'll cut it and come back."

"Great. We thought you'd be a team player," he said, slapping me on the back as I headed toward the door.

I worried that this might happen, and I had already resigned myself to the fact that I may need to trim my fab 'Fro. So I walked home where Mom pulled out her professional-quality scissors and trimmed my hair in our spacious suburban kitchen.

I left the bits of hair on the floor for Mom to clean up and walked back to Burger Beat, scratching my neck the entire way. Back inside, Junior Assistant Manager Tim told me that he and

"higher-ups" still thought it was too long. What sacrifices these people required!

"Okay, fine," I said. "I'll be back in a bit."

I walked home. Mom cut some more. With each snip I pleaded, "Not too much! Not too much!"

I walked back to Burger Beat and, to my astonishment, I was told my 'Fro was *still* too bushy. Tired of walking— and not sure that I was prepared to

Pre-Burger Beat do.

227

alter my persona so drastically just for the privilege of flipping burgers—I told Junior Assistant Manager Tim that I'd come back tomorrow. Maybe. After all, in a way I needed my hair the way Sampson did.

That night, I had a seizure in my bed while listening to "Saturday in the Park" on Chicago's greatest hits album. The Devil danced right into my room. This visit was another biggie, just like those in my old bedroom and in Columbus. Somehow, though, I managed to remain on my bed without crashing to the floor. My head felt as if someone were standing on it, but I felt a bit relieved, vindicated even. I didn't have a seizure problem! Even the best of modern medicine couldn't detect The Evil One, let alone keep him at bay.

I opted not tell Mom and Dad about the seizure, even though they made me swear on my life to tell them if I ever had another one, big or small. But Mom and Dad had enough to worry about. Besides, I didn't want to have to swallow even more pills. A man in my position needed to be energized. I took some aspirin, said some prayers, and went to bed.

The next morning, Mom cut my hair yet some more. I could barely stand to look at my locks as they fell onto the black plastic cape and then slid onto the white linoleum floor. I traipsed back down to Burger Beat and this time was given the thumbs up, the nod, the "get behind the grill" glance from the manager, with Junior Assistant Manager Tim winking behind him.

Life was good.

I was told to report to work—in uniform, of course—the next day at 4:30 P.M. This struck me as odd. Surely 4:30 had to be the start of the dinner rush, the craziest portion of the day. And it was.

On my first day, I was told where to stand and given a device for squeezing just the right amount of ketchup and mustard on the burgers. I was also to toast buns and drop the pale, frozen fish patties into the boiling hot grease.

Requests for me to do this and do that were coming at a rapid-fire pace. Yet I had no idea what I was doing. In orientation it was made clear that we couldn't curse without fear of being fired. Even rudeness was cause for dismissal. We had to plaster smiles on our faces. Worse, every command had to end with a "please" ("A dozen cheeseburgers, *please*") and every acknowledgement had to end with a "thank you" ("A dozen cheeseburgers, *thank you*"). Word was that the owners of Burger Beat were hoping to turn their two small shacks into the next national chain.

Whenever I tried to shoot condiments on the buns, inevitably someone would request more fish. I'd set out to plop the filets into the grease basket, fumbling a few of the patties onto the floor. And then a call would ring out for more toasted buns, *please*.

More experienced employees did their best to help me out. They seemed to have no problem doing three or more things at once, even with people shouting orders—politely—at them. I felt like I was back in little league. *Swing faster! Tighten your grip! Bend at the knees!* And I was performing just as poorly. Maybe worse.

Two-and-a-half hours after its start, my shift ended. I walked home, my uniform wet with sweat and heavily stained with ketchup, mustard, and grease. I inadvertently left the paper hat on my aching head.

The next day at Burger Beat was much the same. The dinner-time rush had me fumbling like Lucille Ball in the chocolate factory. I seemed to put more ketchup and mustard on my clothes than on the buns. I left with another headache. And returned the next day with an even bigger one.

The assistant manager on duty told me that she had heard from other managers and employees that I was difficult to work with. Evidently, in my daze, I sometimes said "give me a sec" and "hold on" to a couple of my colleagues' polite commands rather than the expected "yes, thank you very much, ma'am, it's been my pleasure hearing your request and it will be an even bigger pleasure fulfilling it." This heightened scrutiny increased my stress. I actually performed worse on the third night than on the first.

I began to think more about how my condition—whatever its cause—could really hurt and maybe even kill me.

I thought about the time I went canoeing with my Youth Conservation Corps pals on the Little Miami River. At one point in slow, but deep water, the Devil paddled right alongside me. Afterwards, my head stung, especially when our aluminum canoes scraped the river's rocky bottoms through the shallow rapids. The crunching and grinding sounds clawed up my spine.

I was too cool and too blessed to wear a life vest. Jesus was my life vest. But had the Devil really socked one to me then, I could have easily flipped in the water and drowned. Unless, of course, Jesus was prepared to walk on water again and offer me a helping hand.

It occurred to me in the heat of the third day's condiment comedy that if The Beast struck me at Burger Beat, I could end up face-first on a hot frying surface or, worse, in boiling grease. Today's special: A side order of Fried Steve. Yum.

I walked home thinking of all the other ways my condition could kill me: a car accident, a fall out of a window, drowning in the bathtub. The world's a dangerous place when you have a tendency to blank out.

At home, I found Mom and Dad in the kitchen and matter-of-factly announced that I didn't care for the Burger Beat gig one bit. "I'm going to quit my job," I said. Laying on the drama, I added, "It makes me *really, really* nervous." It was all I had to say. Already worried that I was too stressed out by school, CYO, and now my medical condition, my parents knew I couldn't stand any more anxiety.

Both Mom and Dad were comfortable with my decision. And it freed up more time for me to devote to my pursuit of power. I had managed to get elected the chairperson of the Cincinnati CYO program, somehow beating out a better qualified, smarter, and more sincere kid.

And my sights were now set on a potential run at the national CYO board of directors. If I were to be elected, I would represent Region VI, the thirteen Roman Catholic dioceses of Ohio and Michigan. I would test the waters at a national CYO conference in San Antonio, Texas. My archdiocese chose me to represent them. It was to be my very first plane ride. I couldn't have been more thrilled. It was a long way to San Antonio, so I intended to make a splash. A big one. And indeed I did.

My parents took me to the airport on a Thursday afternoon, I could sense the tension between them, but I was too wrapped up

A piece of my national CYO campaign literature.

in my good mood to care much. They snapped pictures of me at the gate. I insisted that they take one of me talking on a pay phone—an airplane parked on the tarmac in view behind me. I thought that such a shot of a young man on the go, phoning in commands from the airport, could come in handy when it came time to campaign.

Dad slid me a letter, the first I could recall ever receiving from him. It was marked "don't open until twenty-thousand feet." I put it in my carry-on, a canvas Elder gym bag, and forgot about it, too thrilled with my first plane ride. Or maybe too afraid of what it might say.

Once in San Antonio, I took a cab to the diocese's retreat complex. Assuming other kids from other regions also had sights on the national board, I saw the conference as a means of scoping out the competition. While I understood that I was the only one expressing interest in running for the Region VI nomination, I would run against kids from other regions if I decided to seek the national CYO presidency.

Applying the same techniques I used at the Hugh O'Brian conference, I tried to make as many friends as possible from the time the event began on Thursday night. The youth leaders from other dioceses outside my district represented blocs of votes that I could need for my presidential bid. I shook lots of hands. I participated in all the sessions. I asked lots of questions—but not too many. I thought I was making pretty good progress, but my hopes for the national presidency, and a position closer to the papacy, capsized on Saturday afternoon.

We overachievers all went swimming in a nearby community pool. The water was a bit murky, but I was anxious to be the first in—the future leader of Catholic youth nationwide couldn't be intimidated by cold water nor unseen bottoms. Besides, in the pool I could keep my anemic body, any muscle from my running days now gone, under water. Only my 'Fro-topped head would be in view.

I tossed my towel over the fence, secured my swim trunks with a double-knot in the waist tie, and dove with confidence and style—right into the shallow end. I struck the bottom of the pool. With my face.

The rough concrete bottom ripped strips of skin off my forehead, nose, cheeks, and chin like a cheese grater across Baby Swiss. My white legs, nearly as thin as a fire hose, flew up, out of the water, then over my head and back in. For a few seconds—but what seemed like an hour—I floated near the bottom, face up.

Though dazed, I managed to stand, blood dripping off my face, the small globs riding the ripples created by my big splash. I saw, in slow motion, my fellow youth leaders, virtually all still standing around the perimeter. A few pointed at me, horrified looks on their faces. Their mouths moved as if they were yelling, but I couldn't hear much other than a dull ringing. One young lady even looked like she was ready to vomit. I felt like I might.

Someone, I'm not sure who, helped me out the pool and laid me down on a Star Wars beach towel. An adult moderator asked me some questions: my name, the year, my location. I must have scored well on the pop quiz because he didn't call an ambulance. Instead, he picked me up and carried me to his station wagon. He laid me down in the back and then drove back across the street to the retreat complex. He and a couple of other adults helped me clean up. They then laid me down on a couch in an air-conditioned room and told me to rest.

I heard the adults whispering in the hallway, but I couldn't quite make out what they were saying. They were aware of what happened to me in Columbus; my archdiocesan youth director had told them. I lay there wondering what they were thinking, my face feeling as if it had indeed been french-fried.

233

I fought back the tears of pain, embarrassment, and worst of all, certainty that there'd be no presidential bid. What fool would vote for a moron who dove into the wrong end of a pool? Once again, the Devil was up to his old tricks. I would learn later from a doctor that had my trajectory into the pool been slightly different, I could have broken my neck, and maybe even killed myself. Once again, God was looking out for me. Or was he? I had to suffer through the rest of the conference knowing everyone was staring at me. I also had to put up with being the brunt of jokes: *"Hey Steve, does your face hurt? It's killing me!"*

While packing up my clothes—and my dignity—on Sunday morning for the trip home, I found the letter Dad gave me at the airport. I also retrieved the one Mom left for me in my suitcase, which I had also not yet read. I sat on the edge of the bed in my dorm room and read Dad's letter first:

I hope this doesn't sound corny or anything, but I just wanted to say a few things, some of which I never took time to say. First I love you very much and I am proud, like Mom, of all your accomplishments. Your first three years at Elder were great. I am sure the last year will follow true-to-form.

Steve, you ran and beat the best. By "running" I don't necessarily mean running. Continue on and you cannot lose. But don't forget to stand back and have some fun along the way. I don't mean to dampen your time by mentioning any of our family problems, but I am sure your Mom and I can work these problems out. So don't worry, enjoy your trip to Texas.

You will always remember Texas, as Texas, I am sure, will remember you. But have fun along the way.

Love, Dad

P.S. Give 'em hell.

I cried, the tears burning the scrapes on my face. I didn't think there was much hope of those two saving their marriage and our family. I also thought that I'll certainly remember Texas. It will forever be burned into my memory as the place where I lost my face. And my shot at the National CYO presidency.

I then read Mom's note:

I just finished some ironing and some of your packing. I am very happy, even envious of you at this point. I sure wish I was taking this trip. I think we could all use a vacation, some time for thought and peace. I can't give you any guidance as far as the seminary, but you have lots of friends who can help you. As long as I see that you're happy in your life, I'll be happy for you.

Love, Mom

P.S. Don't forget your medicine!

The flight home to Cincinnati was uneventful. I had called Mom and Dad and told them about my accident, but they still weren't prepared to see my face, or lack thereof. Dad shook his head; Mom let out a nervous giggle. I brought back souvenirs for everyone, including, for Uncle Ken, some official Texas bullshit encased in acrylic. I gave J.C. a T-shirt with a beer logo. The shirt, I noticed when I got home, was printed in Cincinnati. "It's the thought that counts," I told him with a smile and a shrug.

The *Catholic Telegraph*, my archdiocese's official newspaper, ran an article about my San Antonio journey. Fortunately, it didn't run with a post-conference photo of my butchered face. The article did note that: "The upsurge in cults, and struggles among teens with divorce, alcoholism, and death, were the subjects of a peer counseling workshop at the conference. This was the session that Steve liked best. 'It helped me to hear from people who have been through these things and realize they weren't crushed by the experiences. It may have been rocky, but they grew.'"

At this point, the Devil only made a visit every month or two. But when he came, he came big. Gone were the short drop-in visits. Now he arrived only if he had bags and intended to stay a while.

Once, while in Michigan for a regional youth ministry conference, I stood up and walked to the elevator to fetch something from my dorm room. I woke up on the floor, a throw pillow under my head. Several people hovered over me, asking how I felt. Or if I needed something to drink. I answered "yes" to both questions, but what I really wanted was for all this seizure stuff to go away. Forever.

Chapter 30

Coming Undone

I made a mental list of all that was now gone: photo frames, knickknacks, and wall hangings, all sorts of tangible things. The inventory, I can now see, was all just a means of avoiding what was really gone. My senior year was going to be one to forget.

In my senior year, two of my favorite priests—Thomas Lenihan and Richard Goins—left the priesthood to marry. I was torn by their decisions, crying openly when Father Thomas announced his decision before me and five other kids assembled at a nearby parish.

I wanted both men to be happy. They deserved to be. Yet I was angry that they were abandoning the life of the cloth, one that I still thought might be in my future (though I was having increasing doubts). I felt a loss for my fellow young people, too. These priests were among a relative few who could really relate to young adults, in a friendly yet mature manner. In turn, those kids could then connect to the church, and to God, through them.

Even more so than the departure of Fathers Thomas and Richard, I was conflicted by my own parents' relationship, in full divorce mode at this point. It was Mom's decision to put an end to the marriage, a strict no-no in the Catholic Church. Though at times I hated her for it, I couldn't really blame her. Not a bit. Living with a drinker can be tough. And I, for one, didn't do much to support her or thank her for all of the many sacrifices she made for the family.

I recall one night shortly before the divorce when Mom scrounged up the money for the two of us to go to the movies, something we had done together only a few times. We hopped in the Beige Bomber. Its windshield sported a huge crack, its bumpers were heavily dented due to a parking brake that sometimes gave out, and on its bald tires we slid part of the way to the theater that rainy night.

Though a dozen shows were available in the megaplex, I lobbied hard to see the one Mom had the least energy for, *Rock Show*, Paul McCartney & Wings in concert. Mom sat through it without complaint, though. And she let me eat more than my fair share of the medium-sized popcorn we shared. Even in the dark, anyone with half a brain—or heart—could have seen that I was a jerk to my own mother. I was too into the music to give a damn.

As I look back on the divorce now, it's clear that Mom had been hanging in there for a while, waiting for her kids to achieve some degree of self-sufficiency before doing something for herself. It's also clear to me now that there are huge demands placed upon a couple married in their teens that immediately starts a family. I passed thirty before having my first child. Had I been only seventeen, my patience and endurance would have been pushed to their limits—and beyond.

My brothers had opted to move out with Mom to a small apartment a few miles away. Teri and I stayed with Dad in our suburban house. What a rough spot for a kid to find himself, torn between his own mother and his church. It sucked. I thought the church's stand on divorce was right, but I also thought that Mom was doing the sensible thing. In an ideal world, I would have had my own place to go and I could have stayed neutral, like Switzerland, in this war.

Mom moved out with Larry and Dave one Sunday. I couldn't bear to watch. Instead, I tossed a football in a park with J.C. and then went to a youth club meeting at St. Teresa in Price Hill. As we walked to J.C.'s car after the meeting, he could tell something was wrong, but he didn't know that this was the day that my family was splitting in two.

J.C. asked what was up and I broke down. We sat on a stone wall on the edge of the parking lot. He hugged me and offered me a cigarette. I wiped the tears off my face and accepted his offer. Moments later, nearly coughing up a lung, I said, "This shit is awful."

"You'll get used to it," J.C. said.

"I'm not going to start smoking."

"I'm talking about the divorce."

"Oh." I took a deep breath to clear my lungs.

"How about a beer?"

"Sounds good to me." J.C. and I picked up a six-pack. We drove to Rapid Run Park and carried our beer to the top of one of the hills I used to run up without breaking a sweat.

"You were the king of this place," J.C. said.

"Not anymore."

J.C. took a big swig of his Hudy Delight, a popular local brew. "Miss running?"

"Now and then."

We sat quiet for a few minutes, the first stars of the evening twinkling above.

"You know your parents still love you, right?"

I could feel the tears coming back. "Yeah, I know."

J.C. put his arm around me. "And I love you too, you skinny freak."

"Screw you," I said. "And give me another cigarette."

We stayed perched atop the hill that had just winded me for an hour. Maybe two. J.C. drank two beers. He let me have four. What a friend, I thought.

When J.C. dropped me off at home I found just a few pieces of furniture: a couch, a coffee table, a couple of kitchen chairs. In our bedrooms, Dad, Teri, and I each had a bed, desk, and chair. I walked around soaking up the emptiness, listening to the quiet as if it were trying to tell me something. I made a mental list of all that was now gone: photo frames, knickknacks, and wall hangings, all sorts of tangible things. The inventory, I can now see, was all just a means of avoiding what was really gone. My senior year was going to be one to forget.

During my final year of high school, the Devil came only once every three or four months, always in the form of a grand mal seizure. Yet, I spent less and less time worrying about, or obsessing over, the battle between good and evil.

Instead, I focused more on church law, especially as it related to divorce, celibacy, and the like. I knew how to plan car washes, give speeches, and read from the Bible at Mass. I knew how to pray, how to thank God for all his blessings. And I knew how to examine my life for the many, many things wrong with it. I didn't, however, know how to respond to a church that seemed to be troubling, belittling, and punishing some of the best people I knew. Myself included.

Several months after the divorce, my priest penpal at the D.C. church wrote me in response to an angst-filled letter I had sent him:

This is a letter that comes full of love, prayers, and sacrifices for you as you struggle in the darkness that seems to strangle the vitality, enthusiasm, and life that comprised last year.

Steve, your pain is real. Divorce hurts and separates, especially those who value family existence as you do. Your family has been shattered, thus causing breakage in you.

I suggest this has unconsciously been brought forward in relation to God, and the Holy Family. You may unknowingly be harboring a deep resentment against God or Joseph as "father" and Mary as "mother" because of your family situation.

My dear friend, don't be one who doesn't allow himself the right to rage, demand, question God, as a son should.

His note struck a chord. I had not done enough raging, demanding, and questioning. And if anyone had the right to expect something from God, it was me. I who offered so much suffering up to him. I who fought the Devil—or at least what I thought was the Devil—for his glory. And for what?

I had certainly been pissed at my earthly father for his transgressions, which at this point were seeming like less and less of a big deal. Perhaps because my own questionable behavior left plenty to be desired.

Besides, my earthly father didn't need any grief. Through the divorce, Dad lost his wife, two of his three sons moved out, and he owned but a couple of measly possessions. He was a walking, breathing country western song.

He hit bottom with even greater force than I struck the shallow end of the swimming pool in San Antonio. But, of course, Dad's wounds were inside, where they hurt more and take more time to heal.

But one good, even amazing, thing came of the divorce: Dad sobered up.

He didn't bother with any hospital detox program. He just went cold turkey, applying the same zealous dedication that he did to his running, juicing—and drinking—to his sobriety. It's an approach that is right only for a few, at best. But it worked for Dad.

It would be years before I would fully appreciate the magnitude and courage of Dad's commitment to sober up. Losing most everything could just as easily have been a reason to drink more. It had been for me.

Dad had stared down his demons. But with all demons—as I most certainly knew—fighting them is an ongoing war, a battle that must be waged day by day. There is no other way.

Even though Dad decided to leave drinking behind, for me coming home every afternoon was often a mixed bag. Dad was usually out, attending a support group. I would do my homework and make phone calls to CYOers, including one of my new girlfriends, Stacey Lange.

Stacey was a volleyball player from Ursuline Academy, an all-girls Catholic school on the east side of town. Infused with a lot of spunk, she was very devoted to the church and full of an amazing, contagious energy.

Despite my feelings for Stacey, I managed to treat her like crap on too many occasions, usually *drunk* occasions. Picking fights and belittling her became my hobby. She was too smart to put up with much of that and dumped me like a non-returnable bottle. Shortly thereafter Stacey and her family moved to Maine.

I can see now how my own drunk behavior mimicked my father's and how the drink did little more than fill me with anxiety over my own insecurities and a false sense of self-importance. Though it would take years to finally get the message, this is the point when a light, faint though it was, began to glow in my mind. It was the light of truth about myself. I usually thought that I was one together kid with boundless potential. In truth, I was insecure, self-centered, and mean-spirited.

Around eight o'clock each night, Dad would come home and say "hello." I'd say "hi" back. I really didn't know what else to say. I wanted to tell him that I was sorry for his losses. I wanted to tell him that he got what he deserved. I wanted to tell him that tomorrow would be better.

But I said nothing. Instead of saying these things, I wrote about them in my high school English journal, which included this letter to Dad: *I can only imagine the hurt you feel after twenty years of a very close, intimate relationship with a wonderful woman. I am willing to share the pain with you. By doing so we can become closer than we ever have. I love you.*

If I could return to that point, I would say and do something that seems so painfully obvious to me now: I would suggest to Dad that we go running.

The exercise would have done us both a world of good.

My appetite would have increased and maybe I would have gained some weight. (I had dropped from 150 to 125 pounds; my waist measured twenty-eight inches, not bad if you're a girl looking for a modeling job). Dad would have burned off some excess nervous energy. I could have alternately praised and questioned God with each stride. Dad could have focused on moving forward, one step at a time.

More than anything, running together would have allowed us to talk more, about our aching legs and lungs, and maybe, just maybe, about our aching hearts, too.

We certainly would have talked about our heroes Ryun, Jenner, Prefontaine, et al. And maybe, just maybe, it would have opened an opportunity for me to tell Dad that he, too, was my hero.

Chapter 31

Nervous Laughter

Only now, as a parent myself, can I imagine

the heartbreak of the moment. But all I could

think about then was what the thrashing on

the floor must have done to my 'Fro.

As expected, I was the only Region VI candidate for the National CYO Federation board, so I did manage to get elected—if you could call it that—in Milwaukee, Wisconsin. My election was made possible in part by my archbishop and spiritual mentor, Joseph Bernadin. I sometimes saw him at the archdiocesan headquarters. Just as I did when near Father Kennedy, I always felt like I was in the presence of a holy man when around Archbishop Bernadin. He wrote me an encouraging letter and contributed twenty-five dollars to my campaign effort.

When a few years later, as a cardinal and archbishop of Chicago, Bernadin was accused of sexual abuse by a former Cincinnati seminarian, I knew in my heart of hearts that it was not true. Unfortunately, I wouldn't have felt so sure of my convictions if the allegation were leveled against some other priests I knew. But, for the record, none ever touched me.

As a member of the National CYO board, I traveled every couple of months to cities around the country to discuss the state of Catholic youth affairs with my fellow board members. I even made a trip to Orange County, California, and, when on a field trip there, stepped into the Pacific Ocean. The best part of that

Archdiocese of Cincinnati

Office of
The Archbishop
100 East Eighth Street
Cincinnati, Ohio 45202
513/421-3131

August 14, 1981

Dear Steve:

Many thanks for your letter of August 11. I am delighted to hear that the recent Archdiocesan Youth Convention was a great success. In particular, I congratulate you as chairman of the Convention. I know that its success was due in large measure to the leadership you gave.

I am also pleased to learn that you are a candidate for office on the NCYOF Executive Board. It is my hope that you will be elected because I know that you will be able to represent Region VI well.

Unfortunately, I shall not be able to attend the fund-raising dinner on August 23 at St. William's. That evening I shall be in Fort Recovery for a Mass for Spanish-speaking migrant workers. However, I am enclosing a check in the amount of $25.00 as a contribution to help with the campaign expenses.

With gratitude for all that you are doing for the Church, and with cordial good wishes, I remain

Sincerely yours in Christ,

Most Reverend Joseph L. Bernardin
Archbishop of Cincinnati

A letter—and check—supporting my national CYO campaign from one of my spiritual heroes: Archbishop Joseph Bernardin.

journey, however, was flying over the Rocky Mountains. I took pictures of the snow-capped peaks from the plane.

At one national board meeting in Philadelphia, I had a full-blown seizure. To keep me from biting my tongue, preppy Tim Clark from North Carolina shoved part of his shirt—a snow-white Izod Lacoste pullover—into my mouth. What Tim had not known was that, as a means of calming my nerves, I had taken to using chewing tobacco. I had placed a wad between my cheek and gum right before the seizure.

When I had stopped convulsing, Tim pulled his shirt out only to see that it now looked like stained underwear. Tim was pissed. I laughed so hard it made my head hurt even worse. It was the first time I could recall actually laughing about my condition.

My fellow board members and I laughed even harder when Linda Borkland from Wyoming shared a book she had found at a garage sale. Called *The Falling Sickness*, it detailed how seizure disorders had been interpreted throughout history. Linda read a few passages aloud. One talked about how the ancient Greeks considered castration a treatment option. Tim, still angry about his shirt, suggested the procedure should begin immediately.

Linda read another excerpt about how, in the eighteenth century, one leading doctor claimed epilepsy could be caused by masturbation. I blushed. Fortunately, Linda quickly jumped to another passage about how, long ago, some thought seizures were the sign of the Devil.

"That's interesting," I said, wanting to know how others would react to the mere suggestion of satanic seizures.

"What morons!" Missy Smyth, a board member from California said, everyone—but me—laughing and nodding in agreement.

"I stubbed my toe yesterday," Tim Clark said. "Maybe the Devil did that to me."

More laughter all around. I couldn't help but join in. It felt good to do so.

I wasn't laughing much around that time. The divorce, the medicine that made me feel tired, and excess rainfall that wreaked havoc on my 'Fro didn't give me much to laugh or feel good about. I was, however, pumped up about the prom. I asked Linda Hemmer, a very smart junior at Seton High School, to go with me. We had known each other through CYO for years and had dated a few times.

For the prom, I carefully picked out a maroon tux. I could still recall the disappointment with my confirmation leisure suit. I didn't want any fashion shortcomings to interfere with this rite of passage.

In the late afternoon of the big day, Dad drove me to the flower shop to pick up a wrist corsage about the size of a basketball. We returned home for my all-important pre-prom primping.

After showering, I put on my underwear, socks, shirt, and pants, and then stood before the bathroom mirror shaping my mane. A transistor radio on top of the toilet played tunes such as "Private Eyes" by Hall & Oates, "Sailing" by Christopher Cross, and, one of my favorites, "Centerfold" by the J. Geils Band.

I probably spent more time on my do than most of the girls who attended that night. It took some doing to get my 'Fro just right: enough fluff to make a statement yet not too much so as to frizz it out. Finding that happy medium took considerable time and skill.

While picking at my hair, the Devil dropped me to the floor. When I came to twenty minutes later and gathered my wits about me, Dad described what had happened. He heard me fall and begin thrashing around, kicking the vanity. He tried to open the door, but I had locked it. (I hated when I was interrupted while working on my curly masterpiece, as it took considerable

247

concentration.) Dad said he pried the door open with a screwdriver and found me stiff as marble on the floor.

Dad had never witnessed an episode before. All those years of hiding my condition from him, Mom—everyone—caught up with both of us that afternoon. It was enough to work Dad into a frenzy, too. Only now, as a parent myself, can I imagine the heartbreak of the moment. But all I could think about then was what the thrashing on the floor must have done to my 'Fro.

I swallowed aspirin, finished dressing, and then called Linda to let her know that I would not likely be up to any heavy-duty boogying, my body too stiff for any Motown moves.

An hour later, when Linda came to pick me up, Dad took a couple of photos, Linda all smiles, me nothing but a grimace. She then

took a photo of me and Dad. In that shot, it's hard to tell from the pained look on both of our faces who just had the seizure.

I met up with two friends and their dates at the prom. I spent most of the night just sitting but toward the

Minutes after a seizure; minutes before my senior prom.

end began to feel better. When the prom was over, Linda and I traveled with the other couples in our group to the Western Bowl bowling alley, one of the few places open after midnight.

My head felt like one of the bowling pins.

I missed Stacey.

I missed Mom and my brothers.

I missed the carefree days at St. William.

I just wanted to put high school behind me.

I had not yet decided where to go to college, or even *if* to go. My two-year term on the National CYO board was certainly going to take a lot of time in the coming year.

On graduation day, Mom, Dad, and Grandma Marge all watched me march into Cincinnati's Music Hall with purple gown and mortarboard. They also watched me walk on stage to collect the Catholic Leadership Award.

The next day, in a move reflective of the true leader I was, I stopped taking my medicine. This was, of course, an amazingly immature thing to do, especially for a recent high school graduate, now supposedly a man.

One month passed without a seizure. Then two, then three. No Devil. I had grown out of the problem, just as the doctors said I might. I postponed college a year, working full-time in a well-paying office job that Dad secured for me.

I saw out my national CYO term, passing on my responsibilities to the next Region VI Representative at the national CYO convention in Washington, D.C.

The Devil stopped visiting altogether.

The following fall I started studying at the College of Mount St. Joseph, a small liberal arts college on the edge of town. As college is apt to make one do, I began to think more critically about my faith. I left it, or more accurately, put it aside. Just years earlier I thought my faith was something I couldn't survive without. And here I found myself at the beginning of a period during which I thought my faith was something I couldn't live *with*.

I was right the first time. It just took me ten years to figure that out.

Among the books I read in college was Milton's *Paradise Lost*. One passage blew me away. Actually, it was just a sentence and it seemed to sum up the better part of my life over the preceding eight or nine years. It read: "The mind is its own place, and in itself can make a heaven of hell, a hell of heaven."

Indeed.

Epilogue

I no longer get Afro perms. And I haven't had a seizure since high school. I am most fortunate that my episodes stopped. Unfortunately, some kids aren't so lucky. I know one such person, my nephew Matthew. Despite his seizures, he manages, like tens of thousands of others with epilepsy, to live a rich, rewarding, and creative life. He's a remarkable young man.

While I do make room in this world for the hand of God and the hand of Satan, I don't believe that run-of-the-mill seizures—mine or others—are the work of the Devil. The mere suggestion is, now, enough to make me laugh. Out loud.

Some have asked if I am angry at my church. "After all," they say, "aren't you pissed at what the church put you through?" To the contrary. I believe the church and my family taught me right from wrong so that, in the bigger picture at least, I ran away from rather than toward the darkness.

I sometimes wonder what would happen if I were a kid experiencing what I did then *today*. Would our seemingly more violent and satanic world lead me to act differently? Would my parents end up on the evening news tearfully explaining that they had no idea what made me snap?

The church also helped me to see—and, later, truly appreciate—the transcendent in my life. And the life of others. Our world is full of mystery and enchantment, among God's greatest gifts. And one for which I am forever grateful.

Today my faith isn't driven by trying to outrun evil and temptation, even though I still need to do some fancy footwork now and then. I now take, or at least try to, a more mature approach to my relationship with God. But I have not abandoned the sense of his power and presence that so shaped my worldview as a child.

My return to the church after a ten-year respite was inspired, in part, by my marriage to Mary Ellen Lacey and the birth of our children: Maggie and Gracie. I enjoy those days when I can meet my kids as they come home from school. I pour them each a cold glass of milk and make peanut-butter-and-jelly sandwiches—on crustless Wonder Bread, of course. And I pray that they tell me *everything* that's on their minds.

The parish that my family calls home is a vibrant church in Deer Park, Ohio, that just so happens to bear my confirmation name: St. John the Evangelist. (Though my heart of hearts and soul of souls is still at St. William on God's Holy Mountain. Always will be.)

While my wife, Mary Ellen, is active in St. John's Church, I have chosen to make contributions from behind the scenes, believing that I had proven long ago that I am not equipped for leadership.

Whatever personal growth I may have managed over the years, it pales in comparison to that of my parents and my childhood pal J.C.

Dad is sober and stays so day by day. We talk several times a week, and see each other often. Dad returned to the church years ago.

Mom has also returned to the church and, with Dad's blessing, has secured an annulment for their marriage. Mom, who has remarried, often attends Latin Mass, no doubt finding it easier to connect with God in the spiritual language of her youth. We, too, talk and visit often. (And it pleases me to tell you that these days she can prepare a meal with the best of them. Miracles never cease.)

Both Mom and Dad are grandparents supreme.

J.C. is the father of two beautiful girls. And like my dad, he lives a sober life and is better for it. We, too, see each other regularly.

Despite the trials and tribulations of my youth, I would not exchange it for another. Perhaps it will seem odd to you, but I would describe my childhood as idyllic. I have my parents, most of all, to thank for that. My only regrets are the too many times that I acted improperly and hurt others, even though I knew better. And I *did* know better.

I thank you again for reading my book. You can share your comments with me at www.stevekissing.com.

Acknowledgments

I would like to thank all of my teachers, advisors, and coaches at St. William, Elder High School, and the College of Mount St. Joseph. I send special thanks to Sister Marjorie, SC; Dave Dabbelt; Tom Bushman; Fran Harmon; Sister Peg McPeak, OSM; and Tom Seibert.

Since taking up writing a few years ago, I have been fortunate to receive lots of helpful criticism—and a bit of encouragement—from true pros: Kathy Doane, Mike Maul, David McCumber, Kitty Morgan, Rick Segal, and Paul Singer. I'd especially like to thank Pete Fromm, a writer of mind-blowing talent.

My many deficiencies as a writer should not reflect poorly on the aforementioned mentors, but rather on my own intellectual and artistic shortcomings.

I remain most appreciative of Father Kennedy and his flock at St. William's Church during the 1960s, '70s, and early '80s. The parish was a wonderful place where people lived God's commandment to love one another. I trust it's the same way today.

I thank my doctors who cared for me in a sage and sensitive manner. There's a special place in heaven for physicians like them who can, with real grace, treat frightened children *and* comfort worried parents.

Writing a book while a spouse, a parent, and an employee inevitably means that one's mate, children, and colleagues sometimes get the raw end of the deal. So, from the very bottom of my heart, I thank my beautiful and amazing wife, Mary Ellen, and my two delightful kids, Maggie and Gracie. They make my life so wonderful and complete. I also send thanks to my wonderful colleagues at Barefoot Advertising for their support and encouragement. I especially thank the company's partners, Doug Worple, Fran Dicari, and John Yengo. They allowed me to modify my schedule based on the demands of my book-writing life.

I also want to thank five people who were kind enough to read my draft manuscript and share their insightful comments. They are: Barbara Conry, Peg Halpin, Amy Malcom, Mike Seibert, and Scott Whittington.

My agent, Linda Roghaar, held my hand and guided me through the tumultuous experience of selling a book in today's competitive and chaotic publishing environment. I am in her debt.

Every writer dreams of someone who has unbridled passion for his work. Carol Brown was my dream come true. A book business veteran, she selflessly went out of her way to see that my book found a great home. And it did: Crossroad Carlisle Books. Thank you so much, Carol!

I was fortunate to have found a great editor, too: Roy M. Carlisle. Without him, this book would be a mere shadow of its current self. Every writer should be so fortunate to have an editor with such skill, patience, and insight. I thank God that I found Roy. He's the best.

My copyedtior, Dorian Gossy, was most meticulous. I am so glad that my manuscript ended up in front of her eagle eyes. I'm also pleased that Margaret Copeland designed the pages you've seen here, making my words look their absolute best. And I'd also like to thank John Eagleson for proofing these pages.

And since books don't sell themselves, I'm grateful that John Jones and Maria Devitt are part of The Crossroad Publishing

Company. Their enthusiasm for my work and their sales and marketing know-how filled me with much confidence. And hope that someone besides my family and friends would buy the book.

Assisting in this book's cover design and the creation of its promotional materials were some of my colleagues at Barefoot Advertising: Jeff Chambers, Susan Davidson, Sara Eames, Adam George, Charlie Padgett, David Schlosser, David Valentine, and Doug Worple. Special thanks are owed to Carey McGuire and Jodi Greene, two young women of exceptional talent. Also providing help were T.J. Vissing and Allison Stettler of OMS Photography. They're responsible for the great image on the cover of this book. What a blessing to have such artistic, talented friends.

I thank my mom and dad, again, for supporting me in this and every other endeavor. They have been—and continue to be—far better parents than I have been a son.

There have been many more influential people in my life than this short tale would allow me to include. So I thank all of my friends and family and say: If you didn't find yourself here, it doesn't mean that you weren't—and aren't—important to me. You know better. And so do I.

About the Author

Steve Kissing is an award-winning advertising copywriter and a contributing editor to Cincinnati Magazine. His writing has won awards from the American Advertising Federation and the Society of Professional Journalists, among others. He lives in Cincinnati, Ohio, and, these days, is possessed only by family and fly fishing.

Steve can be reached through his website: www.runningfromthedevil.com

The text face is URWPalladio.
The headings are set in Minya Nouvelle.

OTHER TITLES OF INTEREST

C. McNair Wilson
RAISED IN CAPTIVITY
How to Survive (and Thrive in) a Religiously Addicted Family

Actor and humorist McNair Wilson is back with his first new book in over two decades. In this hilarious memoir, he pokes fun at everything from Sunday School to strict sexual mores.

0-8245-2118-8 $16.95 paperback

Carmen Renee Berry
WHEN HELPING YOU IS HURTING ME
Escaping the Messiah Trap
REVISED AND UPDATED!

Carmen Renee Berry. Best known as the co-author of the million-selling *girlfriends,* first appeared on the national scene with the publishing phenomenon that started everyone talking about The Messiah Trap and how to overcome it. With her unsurpassed ability as a writer and teacher, Berry shows how we can only help others once we learn to love ourselves.

0-8245-2108-0 $16.95 paperback

OTHER TITLES OF INTEREST

 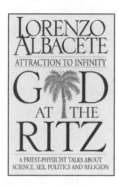

Dana Sawyer
ALDOUS HUXLEY
A Biography

"I highly recommend Dana Sawyer's biography of Aldous. It is authentic, clearly written, and fascinating. I couldn't stop reading it." —Laura Huxley, Founder and President of Children: Our Ultimate Investment

In this accessible new biography, Sawyer explores Huxley's life and the impact it had on his writings—including his classic, *Brave New World*.

0-8245-1987-6 $19.95 paperback

Lorenzo Albacete
GOD AT THE RITZ
Attraction to Infinity

A Priest-Physicist Talks About Science, Sex, Politics and Religion

"God at the Ritz deals with the most awesome experiences of life. These experiences propel the human search for truth, beauty, justice solidarity, and personal development. They confront us with the great Mystery that always lies beyond..."—From the Introduction

A prominent priest and columnist for *The New York Times Sunday Magazine* offers his commentary on a variety of topics where current events and pop culture touch the spiritual: the recent bombings at the World Trade Center, the Chicken Soup series, Germaine Greer, and Charles Darwin, among others.

0-8245-1951-5 $19.95 hardcover
0-8245-2113-7 $16.95 paperback Spanish Edition

OTHER TITLES OF INTEREST

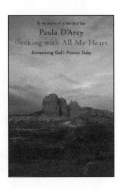

Birell Walsh

PRAYING FOR OTHERS

Powerful Practices for Healing, Peace, and New Beginnings

In the tradition of Larry Dossey's *Prayer is Good Medicine* comes this healing, holistic book on a topic little covered on bookshelves or in the media. *Praying for Others* weaves together prayer success stories from a variety of faith traditions, including Zen, Cabala, Sufism, and Christianity, along with Walsh's own journey toward wholeness through prayer. In the course of the book, he introduces readers to a number of contemporary people who have devoted their lives to praying for others.

0-8245-1949-3 $16.95 paperback

Paula D'Arcy

SEEKING WITH ALL MY HEART

Encountering the Presence of God in the Bible and Christian Literature

A verse in Jeremiah promises that the seemingly elusive God will be found when "you search for me with all your heart". This collection of reflections and meditations is such a search—a search that has taken D'Arcy through both New and Old Testament, honored writings, as well as the reaches of her own experience. D'Arcy shows contemporary spiritual seekers that when we meditate on these verses, our sense of time disappears and there is only now.

0-8245-2109-9 $19.95 hardcover

OTHER TITLES OF INTEREST

Henri Nouwen
Edited by Michael Christensen and Rebecca Laird
THE HEART OF HENRI NOUWEN
Selected Readings

Henri Nouwen is considered one of the greatest spiritual writers of our day, and is without questions one of the best selling, with titles such as *Life of the Beloved* and *In the Name of Jesus* to his name. He taught at Harvard, Yale, and Notre Dame. To commemorate the 70th anniversary of Nouwen's birth, Crossroad is issuing this remarkable anthology of the best of the writings of Nouwen, along with insights from people who knew him in person. Key themes in these writings include: a personal relationship with God, suffering and living for others.

0-8245-1985-X $18.95 hardcover

Please support your local bookstore, or call 1-800-707-0670.

For a free catalog, please write us at:
The Crossroad Publishing Co.
481 Eighth Avenue, Suite 1550, New York, NY 10001
Please visit our website at www.crossroadpublishing.com

All prices subject to change.